CHRISTIAN AT THE CROSSROADS

CHRISTIAN AT THE CROSSROADS

KARL RAHNER

A Crossroad Book
The Seabury Press · New York

The Seabury Press
815 Second Avenue
New York, N.Y. 10017

Published originally under the title
Wagnis des Christen
© Verlag Herder KG, Freiburg im Breisgau,
Federal Republic of Germany, 1974
English translation © Search Press Limited, 1975

The translation was made by V. Green

Library of Congress Catalog Card Number: 75-29634
ISBN: 0-8164-1204-9

Printed in Great Britain

Contents

Foreword   **7**

1 FUNDAMENTALS

1 What is man?   11
2 Why am I a Christian?   21
3 The core of the faith   31
4 What is truth?   37
5 What is evangelization?   40

2 PRACTICE

1 The sword of faith   45
2 The possibility and necessity of prayer   48
3 Is prayer dialogue with God?   62
4 The *Exercises* today   70
5 Penance and confession   75
6 Lent   81
7 The theology of dying   84
8 Hope and Easter   87
9 The future   94

Foreword

For many Christians the present period of change in the Church is very upsetting. Some feel that a cosy home has fallen about their ears. They find themselves on the inhospitable street. Others feel that the Church is crawling into the future at a snail's pace, and they become restive. In this situation, dialogue sometimes seems impossible and irrelevant in the daily life of the Church. We must hope that an awareness of essentials will foster the spirit of community which, despite differences of opinion, will continue to bring (or keep) people together.

These texts are concerned with such essentials. The questions asked are about the basic content of the faith in theory and practice. I have tried to present the faith to the man of today in such a way that he cannot, on the basis of his own convictions, dismiss it as ideology or myth. I deal throughout with the actual practice of human life. Hence my first question: What is man?

The Christian venture is the same for all Christians, whatever their chosen path to fulfilment. They must gradually mature into that hoping love and loving hope in which they can completely lose themselves in God. It is only in this existential selflessness that they will be free to serve the world. Having lost themselves, they can stir others to that love which in the end distinguishes the Kingdom of God from every other communal utopia.

KARL RAHNER

I
FUNDAMENTALS

1 What is man?

What do we mean by man? My reply, stripped to its essentials, is simple: Man is the question to which there is no answer. It is true that everyone goes through a large number of experiences in the course of his life. Drawing on those experiences, he gains knowledge about himself. It is also true that there are a large number of human sciences whose findings on man are continually growing. There is a metaphysical and even a theological science of man, and I am far from saying that it is all foolishness or uncertainty. On the contrary. However:

What is the situation with regard to our own experiences (including their extensions in reading poetry, looking at paintings and so on)? We go through them and then promptly forget about them. We have experiences and later we lose our understanding of the conditions which made them possible and we are unable to live them through again. Experiences should be lessons from the past for the future. However, the old situations in which they arose do not recur.

What do we really know about our earlier experiences? When we try to sort, evaluate, arrange and reduce them to some sort of system, even in our own minds, we undergo a sceptical self-mistrust—one of the least trustworthy of feelings. We are afraid that this whole assessment of life's experiences is too much a prey to ill-thought-out prejudices—'pre-judgments'—for us to have clear or certain knowledge about ourselves. When we hear others speak of *their* experiences (with all the selectiveness, arbitrariness and narrowness of which they are capable), we fear for our own experiences. We notice that each one of us makes his 'own' experiences, and only those. Yet we all want them to be in some way 'objective'. And what do we really know about ourselves, once we have experienced how limited our own experiences are, how much 'arranged' they are by our own freedom (which we

can never 'knowingly' grasp), and that they mean the renunciation of experiences which we could have had but did not have.

Who can say with certainty that he does not use his 'experiences' (which are always at the mercy of a man's unconscious
manipulation) to deceive himself about himself? We have all experienced the fact that we are still a question to which we can
give no answer on the basis of our own lives (as a collection of
experiences). Experience gives answers, but no answer which
would make what we are questioning—man as a unity and as a
whole—intelligible. (It is not my purpose here to inquire into
whether this one, all-embracing question is really directed at the
intelligibility of man, or whether this intention does not indicate
the basic error as to the proper goal of this fundamental question,
and therefore as to man who is this question.)

And what about the conclusions of the natural sciences? Much
of the answer to this question is expressed in our thoughts on 'experience', because ultimately these sciences are no more than the
systematically acquired results of man's experience. Once it is
established that these can give no answer to the question that is
ourselves, the same may be said in advance of whatever is sub-
sequently affirmed about them. Do not misunderstand me: all
praise to those sciences. If I am successfully operated on for ap-
pendicitis, if a sleeping-tablet induces peaceful sleep, if I need no
longer live like Neanderthal man, if I can watch a football match
in California by satellite; and if we can honestly say that we are
not willing to forgo all this, despite our protests against consumer
society, outrages and injustice, if therefore we affirm it, then of
course we are profiting by those sciences. We praise them with our
lives; we should not revile them with our mouths. Also the re-
search they pursue can bring with it, in itself and not just because
of the vital uses it discovers in things, a commendable euphoria of
discovery and knowledge, even an aesthetic enjoyment. But do
they give an answer to *the* question, or just an answer to questions? (Later on I shall reply to the objection that this distinction
between question and questions is a nonsense, that over and above
the sum of questions there is no further question over which man
need trouble either his heart or his head.) The pluralism of these
sciences is insuperable, and hence no answer can be extracted
from their answers. By insuperable I mean that the findings of
these sciences cannot be combined into a comprehensive 'formula
of man' of which all particular findings would be merely applications and special cases, because the 'psychic' (which is certainly a
part of man) cannot be reduced to the 'physical', however much it
may be the business of the human sciences to examine the unity

(not identity) of spirit and matter and throw an increasingly penetrating and permanent light on it. This fundamental irreducibility exists because an identity of spirit and matter—if such there were —would still be an identity in thought, an identity in the thought of a subject; the thought of unity and the unity that is thought of would still be two different things, even if we could reduce everything to thinking and even if we could understand the content of thinking as a merely dependent function of thinking, which the 'realists' of the modern natural sciences are least willing to do.

Further, because of the limitations of my IQ, the restricted time at my disposal for learning and my freely chosen range of interests (as I emphasize this or that), the sum of all the human sciences cannot be accommodated in 'my' (a single individual's) mind. A computer does not help, although it can be fed with vastly more knowledge than my brains. The computer is quite indifferent to the 'knowledge' fed into it, and only a limited amount can be transferred to my brains even when the computer is fully programmed. Ultimately only the knowledge 'stored up' by me from the computer is of significance to me. All I am left with is a very limited and ultimately a very arbitrary choice from everything that the human sciences might know 'in themselves'. Presumably 'other' knowledge—knowledge which is 'out there' but not in my head—is used by others only so that they can control me without my noticing or being able to guard against it. And even supposing that the sum of all these sciences were in my head, they would still be only in *my* head as *my* thoughts, arranged by *me* and used by *me* as a free subject. This subject of freedom— this free individual—would know of its own basic decisions (which can never be the adequate object of reflexion, because reflexion is always itself in the concrete, an act of freedom) nothing distinct and nothing exhaustive. The sum of scientific answers would, if they were the content of the free individual's thought processes, frame an unanswered question. And we can add, for the person who does not fully appreciate this, that in any case all these sciences are still 'on the way'; they have more questions than answers. Even today the sum of the questions seems to grow faster than the sum of the answers. Therefore today's short-lived I —I who cannot wait for the infinitely extended future of the sciences (in which everything in any case would still be finitely clear), or console myself with this future in the obscurity of present-day science—am in actual fact and inescapably the subject who receives more questions than answers from the science which is really accessible to *me*.

What, finally, do we notice about metaphysics and man—about

metaphysical anthropology? If it has a correct understanding of man, then it must grasp him as the essence of an unlimited transcendentality, as the subject who goes beyond (and in going beyond, creates himself as spirit) each individual (finite) object; as the being who can nowhere come to a final standstill. But this infinite extent of possible knowledge, insights and experiences never reaches total fulfilment from within itself and with the means at its disposal. The space or 'warehouse' in which experience, life, knowledge, happiness, pain and so forth are stored is infinite, and so is always half empty (a generous estimate!).

Because we reach out beyond each finite object, but directly grasp only finite objects even if we had never done with finite time, every end is just a beginning. Hence the horrible tedium of it. We are constantly feeding new material into the warehouse of our consciousness. It constantly disappears into an infinite expanse which, not to put too fine a point on it, is just as empty as before. Our experience is like that of the man on a fixed bicycle: he pedals until he is ready to burst, but stays on the same spot.

It is easy to say that every moment of life offers something of beauty and that we should enjoy the present hour as it comes, without attempting to see beyond it. Anyone who takes this as a working principle has only to try it to find it doesn't work. At least once in his life that 'beautiful' moment is filled with the emptiness of death. The anticipation of man's transcendental nature beyond every individual thing (in which he has the impression of reaching forwards into the void) is sometimes a part of that spiritual dying which in 'biological' death is inevitable, even for the least sensitive. Why should we ever wish to hide it from ourselves?

At this point we are not looking at a 'beyond' of which philosophy has nothing to say. In our lived existence, our acquired knowledge is a process extended in time. And our time is finite and ends with death, which is always close. In such finite time as this, the only product of a process of knowledge extended in time is a finite knowledge. We see that quite clearly: the progress of knowledge means only that we experience all the more vividly the infinitude and permanent non-fulfilment of our questioning. The spirit's pride in never needing to come to a final standstill is also its ever sharper pain at never really getting there. We may, of course, dismiss this philosophy of transcendentality permanently unfulfilled in this life as mere fancifulness. Or we may assert that today it could hardly be called modern; or that such transcendentality is no more than the impulse behind the particular knowledge of the individual, in which function it has fulfilled its purpose without being able to lay any claims to significance in itself.

Nevertheless, this unfulfilled transcendentality remains, even though it may be pushed to one side. It is at work behind countless phenomena of individual and collective life: in boredom, the mists of which swallow up the variety of real life; in aggressive irritation at the present because it comes at us with such intolerable incompleteness that we are tempted to flee it into a kind of utopian dreamworld of the future; in psychological attempts to escape a world which seems (with every justification) too narrow and desolate; in the attempt to enhance or raise the finitely pleasant or finitely significant into pure enjoyment or an ideology; in the hope that the phenomenon of the finiteness of all these enhanced realities will cease to make its presence felt; in the attempt to overcome radical evil by acquiring an infinitude which will give us something more than the inevitably finite good; and so on.

I am not trying to maintain that it is impossible to drug oneself against the pain of transcendentality's non-fulfilment. Is any drug effective, however, in *all* the situations of life? And even if it should be, would its user not be freely opting for man's definitive unhappiness? Isn't damnation the freely-chosen, definitive situation of the 'bourgeois' who has no interest in the unattainable? In the past, the evil which led to damnation could be lived only in actions which even in the realm of immediate experience were worked out as destruction and pain. Today, real evil can be lived out in 'middle-class' normality in so far as that normality limits itself to the normal and attainable, rejects the sacred utopia of absolute hope as stupidity, and ultimately reaps its own punishment: condemnation to eternal narrowness. The philosophy of unlimited transcendentality makes man an unlimited question without its own answer. It reflects only what the experience of life and the human sciences already experience and suffer, and expresses the actuality of these experiences in their inner necessity.

What am I to say about faith and theology? Surely *they* promise a fulfilment of man's infinite capacity with the eternal 'possession' of God who bestows himself, without any creaturely mediation, in his very own reality, just as he is, in and for himself? Yes, they do, and that is man's sacred hope. But this hope must be rightly understood. Faith and theology *also* assert that even in eternal beatitude God remains the inconceivable. How could it be otherwise? If God were conceived in this blessedness, he would be circumscribed, and man's transcendentality would reach out beyond God and triumph over God and turn itself into God. How, then, can God the inconceivable be man's goal and happiness?

How (to turn the question round) is man to be conceived if this inconceivable God is his happiness?

There is no easy answer to this, because the conception of what is inconceivable is a knowledge that cannot be calculated on other forms of knowledge and *their* comprehensibility. Understanding that one does not understand is a peculiar form of knowledge; it cannot be an isolated case on the margin of understanding to be totted up with other forms of understanding. Either an understanding of non-understanding does not exist because it is self-contradictory, or it must be the most fundamenal form of understanding on which all other forms of conception depend. The anticipation of transcendentality beyond the totally conceivable (apparently into the void) must also be the supportive precondition of the understanding of God's inconceivability in the beatific vision. The vision must be the most radical and inevitable experience of God's incomprehensibility, and *therefore* the fulfilment of man's transcendentality towards the uncircumscribable. The inconceivability of God in the vision must be understood not as the mere index of creaturely knowledge's finitude, as the buffer at which that knowledge is brought up short, but as the very 'impletion' of its inner dynamism. If that is correct, the essence of knowledge itself is in fact changed: it takes on another essence for which incomprehensibility is no longer a limit that rebuffs but, precisely as incomprehensibility, the very object of its search.

The dry statement of God's incomprehensibility even in immediate vision is apt to puzzle most men and Christians. They think that the beatific vision will supply enough knowledge and perception to make them happy for eternity. They also say that once we see God, all the riddles and inconceivable things in life will dissolve into radiant brightness and clarity, and that eternity is there for us to see that God has made everything good. These Christians forget, however, that we cannot divide in God the incomprehensible from the perceptible, that what is seen is precisely what is incomprehensible, that this is true not only of the 'essence' of God but also of his free decisions disposing of our life and so of our eternity, that the sting of incomprehensibility (it could have been different, why was and is it just so and not otherwise for all eternity?) is not pricked out of our hearts, but will be experienced and felt with burning clarity in the vision of God as eternally valid, without there remaining the possibility of delusion or the faintest possibility that it will one day change. In Christian teaching, beatitude is the everlasting and irrevocable vision of God's inconceivability and therefore also (because it is grounded on the inconceivability of God's freedom) of our own inconceivability to ourselves.

Is it not true, then, that man is a question to which there is no answer? If the answer to this question is Yes, then of course by the 'answer' which is not, is meant an answer in which one fact is understandable as the compelling consequence of another, which itself (because there is no progression into infinity) is 'understandable' simply in and by itself, which is to say ... Yes, what exactly is it to say? How far will individual realities 'lead back?' And what is it to which, *ex supposito*, they do lead back? What does it mean to say that something must be understandable in itself and therefore necessary? We say this of God. But are we not really saying that this ultimate reality is inconceivable? (Why do we not say 'incomprehensible'? Would it not be the same thing, and do we find it embarrassing to use the longer word 'incomprehensible' for fear that we shall notice the goal of our conception's journey, namely the incomprehensible?)

If, however, there is to be an 'answer' to the unanswerable question which is man, then it can consist only in heightening, not in answering, this question; in conquering and piercing the dimension in which the question is posed in the way to which all questioning must conform; therefore it must itself remain an unanswerable question.

To cut a long story short (I could not in any case make it very long, because the real 'answer', which does not and never can exist, cannot be derived from the question, and because therefore our only course, when we have come to an end of the hitherto existing dimension of the question into understanding, is a leap into what is totally other); and in view of the inconceivability which makes an answer impossible: we must renounce any such answer, not experience this renunciation as in the least painful (otherwise where would our beatitude be?). We must let ourselves go into this inconceivability as into our true fulfilment and happiness, let ourselves be taken out of ourselves by this unanswered question. This incomprehensible venture, which sweeps all questions aside, is customarily referred to as the (devout) love of God. Only that turns darkness into light. By 'love' in this context, we are not to understand something the meaning of which we could grasp by comparison with other things. Instead we are to accept this description of letting ourselves go into the inconceivable (whereby the letting go is at once destiny and act, and therefore free and willing) as the definition of love from which this word love takes its significance. (I am not inquiring here into how what we usually experience as and call 'love' contains a part of what I understand by love here.)

'St Teresa says of Satan that "he does not love",' writes Montherlant. That is correct, and reveals the essence of damnation. The damned do not love and do not wish to love for eternity, and look for happiness in being dispensed from having to let themselves go into God's inconceivability. Satan believes he loses nothing by not seeing God, because in the logic of definitive guilt guilt dispenses us from having to contemplate (=love) inconceivability, which we hate because by definition it does not surrender to us. Love, however, is the surrender by which we definitively relinquish control of ourselves and of everything else. For the man who loves and knows what love is, the loveless man is damned.

If we wished to call the attempt to do without the inconceivability of love and the beloved 'happiness' (one of many possible forms of happiness!), even Satan would be happy. He 'understands' himself only as *he* wants to, relying on the alternative to selfless love, which is the effort towards self-assertion and autonomy. The man who loves has escaped this unhappiness, because in his loving leap into one alternative (the acceptance of God's inconceivability) he has put the other alternative (isolated self-possession) behind him.

Man is the unanswerable question. His fulfilment and happiness are the loving and worshipping acceptance of his inconceivability and unanswerability, in the love of God's inconceivability with which we can learn to 'cope' only by the practice of love and not by the theory of the desire to understand. (How could Aquinas say that the essence of happiness consists in an act of the intellect, when he knew that God is inconceivable; when he prayed: 'I worship you, O hidden Godhead', and knew that in the vision God's inconceivability does not disappear. It comes to the light of eternity so radically and irrevocably that either we must travel to hell where, at least on the surface, one has no more to do with this inconceivability, or we must ourselves go with the happy despair of love into the inconceivablity of God?)

Many people think they know where they stand: in themselves, in their society, in their life, or in their mission. Of course we know a lot about all these things. And why shouldn't these insights be our food and escort on the road to the inconceivability of ourselves and of God? But we notice increasingly how all knowledge is really only the road to (known and accepted) inconceivability; that the proper essence of knowledge is love in which knowledge goes out of itself and man lets himself go willingly into inconceivability.

We can cope with the incomprehensibilities of life only if we do not try to master them with that philistine foolishness which often passes for brave lucid wisdom. In that way we can accept the fact that all the single insights of life (however modest, ambitious, loving, unsentimental, industrious, critical, 'positive', intelligent and so forth they may be) will never form a whole. We do not then imagine that there could be a well-tempered synthesis of all these disparate insights which could cater for them all.

All that I have said about man might strike the reader as being very abstract and pale. But the more exact and comprehensive physics becomes, the more obscure and abstract it is. And it is correct, even though only a minority understand it and yet conduct their lives by laws they do not understand. The same may be said of a theory about man's true essence. It makes sense to think about it, and most people in day to day practice conform with this essence even though they do not understand it 'theoretically'. That does not matter, because this theoretical essence is not theory but love surrendering to the inconceivable (which is the denial of theory). Therefore we may be man without 'knowing' it, because true knowledge even of one who knows can be gained only when he resigns his knowledge in favour of the blessed and eternal *docta ignorantia*, or ignorance of the wise.

Yet how simple Christianity is. It is the determination to surrender to the inconceivability of God in love; the fear that one does not do this, but instead draws a line at the comprehensible and so sins; the belief that Jesus managed to achieve this surrender and in doing so was definitively accepted by the one who enabled him to achieve it; the belief that in achieving this surrender in Jesus God has irrevocably promised himself to us as well.

A Christian is a true and most radical sceptic. If he really believes in the inconceivability of God, he is convinced that no individual truth is really true except in the process (which necessarily belongs to its real essence) in which it becomes that question which remains unanswered because it asks about God and his inconceivability. The Christian is also a man who can cope with this otherwise maddening experience in which (to formulate it with poor logic but accurate description) one can accept no opinion as wholly true or wholly false.

Anyone who in a hasty reading finds the above foolish and superficial should pause to consider that in any objection he might be tempted to offer, he is elaborating the only alternative with an empty No, and so lets it reach into the void. This reach is in fact the first act of openness to the inconceivability of God, the invitation and grace to accept it and in this acceptance to find one's own inconceivability.

2 Why am I a Christian?

The following reflexions are written by one who is not 'neutral' but 'committed', by one in other words who hopes he is a Christian to the best of his ability. The ultimate questions of life can in fact be expressed only by a committed person, because, in so far as they are questions embracing everything as a totality, they have no standpoint outside themselves. If one were to suggest the opposite, one would be misunderstanding the object of the question. The subjective (which is not the same as the subjectivistic) is the only way of access into the objective.

I am therefore going to attempt to describe what I mean and try to live out when I say that I should like to be a Christian. We have to say, 'I should like to be,' because in our Christian self-understanding we must ultimately leave it entirely to God whether we are truly what we intend to be and also, of course, what we are socially and ecclesially.

I should like to be a man who is free and who can hope; who understands, and lives as if he understood, that he is entrusted to his own freedom which fulfils itself in life and ultimately makes of him what he has been pregiven as the pattern of true manhood: a man of loyalty, love and responsibility. I am convinced that such a history of real, free self-determination is found in all the impenetrability, questioning, helplessness, ineptitudes and beginnings without tangible endings which go to make up our lives; that therefore the historical life of man in freedom is directed towards a point of absolute decision, and conceals such a decision within itself; that life as a totality must ultimately be accounted for and not simply dispersed in the void in all these particular things.

Naturally, philosophers and other theorists of human life can reflect on such concepts as freedom, responsibility, love, selflessness, until the cows come home; these concepts are not immediately clear and transparent to me either; but they do have a meaning and give direction to one's own decision in the thousand trifles of life. It might be thought that one could analyze such words psychoanalytically, biologically, sociologically and expose them as the (avoidable or unavoidable) superstructure of much more primitive things which would then count as the only true realities. But because in all such attempts it is the same subject at work, with his responsibility, such attempts at analysis are, for me at any rate, false.

I cannot and have no wish to evade this freedom for which I as a true subject am responsible. I accept myself. I accept myself without protest with all the conditions and contingencies of my biological and historical existence, even though I have the right and duty to change and improve in it whatever seems to me to be an encumbrance. Even so it remains opaque, burdensome, not soluble into mastery-giving transparency, short and full of pain and helplessness. I accept it in hope as it is; in the one hope which embraces and supports everything, of which we never know whether we really have it; in the hope that this incomprehensibility (with all its palpable beauty) will one day be revealed in its ultimate meaning and that that meaning will be both definitive and blessed.

Who will convince me that all this is utopian; that it is false and cowardly, worse than if I embraced radical scepticism, which is theoretically possible but never sustained in the reality of a life in which responsibility is borne and welcomed? Of course this ultimate and basic confidence in the total and all-embracing meaning of existence is not an unattached ideology: not only does everything else depend on it, but it also depends on everything else that life offers, because in it the Christian finds (at least partially) the experience of meaning, light, joy, experienced love and fidelity, all of which make an absolute claim. Something more must be said later about these concrete experiences (or at least one of them) which underscore one's ultimate hope as they are underscored by it.

However, the free fundamental act of existence which I have just tried to express in halting words concerns that which, or better the one whom, we call God. I know that this is a vague term. I know that the reality it denotes can be found in a man's life even when the word itself is not. I know that today the reality is not easy to realize when presented as a great cosmic builder (as in the time of the Enlightenment). I know that much mischief is worked by this word because so many atrocities and fatuities have been justified in God's name. But I say, nevertheless, that I call the ultimate ground of my hope, in the act of unconditioned acceptance of my existence as meaningful, 'God'. This is not to turn him into the projection of my hope into a void, for on the one hand, in the very moment I think of God as *my* projection, 'God' becomes meaningless and ineffective in my life, and on the other, I cannot renounce the ground of my hope any more than I can renounce my hope. God must be the ultimate reality which supports and embraces everything if he is to be the ground and goal of my hope as expressed in the confident, radical acceptance of existence.

This God, however, is the inconceivable mystery in oneself, for this hope (in which reason and freedom are still one) goes beyond all that can be given, in so far as every particular thing that can be grasped, intelligibly thought of and set up as a signpost in one's assessment of life is always determined and threatened by other things and remains threatened. The act of acceptance of existence in confidence and hope is therefore, rightly understood, the act of letting oneself go into the inconceivable mystery.

My Christianity is therefore, rightly understood, the act of letting myself go into the inconceivable mystery. My Christianity is consequently anything but an 'explanation' of the world and my existence: it is rather the injunction not to regard as definitive, as completely intelligible in itself, any experience or any understanding (however beneficial and enlightening it might be). The Christian has less 'ultimate' answers which he could throw off with a 'now the matter's clear' than anyone else. He cannot use his God as *one* discovered signpost in the assessment of his life, but only in silence and adoration accept him *as* the incomprehensible mystery, and *that* as the beginning and end of his hope and therefore as his sole definitive and all-embracing salvation.

In so far as the Christian knows that this radical confidence of his is based on God himself, he calls this most intimate movement of his existence to God and by God's grace, the 'Holy Spirit', and articulates this one movement on the strength of the immediacy of God as grace, hope and love. To every man who is true to the verdict of his conscience, a Christian concedes this innermost movement into God by means of God, even though that man does not yet reflect it as such and cannot yet grasp its historical appearance in Jesus Christ in the reflexion of an explicit Christian faith. A Christian is afraid that he (and *therefore* also others) might in freedom refuse this innermost movement of his existence by grace in explicit or latent unbelief and lack of hope in his life; but he hopes that in others and *therefore* also in himself this movement will find its definitive, 'eternal' goal despite all the darkness and superficiality of life.

A Christian accepts the ultimate threat to his existence that arises from the fact that his freedom can deny itself, and again and again averts it by the hope that the history of man's freedom, which is embraced by the freedom of the incomprehensible mystery, will on the whole, through God, have a blessed outcome, even though no theoretical statement can be deduced as to the salvation of any particular individual.

All that has been said so far, however, has, for me, the Christian, been mysteriously synthesized in the encounter with Jesus of Nazareth, in a synthesis in which this basic hope and the experience of Jesus condition and justify each other mutually in an ultimately indissoluble reciprocity in the intellectual conscience of a man who wants to be honest—but in an intellectual honesty which also embodies what we Christians call 'humility'. Mediated by the message of Christianity and the Church in the Gospel of Jesus *and* encouraged by that ultimate hope in the power of grace, the Christian meets Jesus. As whom does he meet him?

To answer this question we can take various aspects of the experience; here, therefore, the way of describing the content of the encounter with Jesus will not be the only possible and therefore universally binding one. The experience is always conditioned by the totality of its moments as a whole. In Jesus we see a man who loves, who is faithful even to death, in whom the whole of human existence, life, speech, activity is open to the mystery he calls his Father, to whom he therefore trustingly surrenders even when his world collapses. For him the unfathomable, the obscure abyss of his life is the saving hand of the Father. And so he holds on to his love for men and to his hope even when everything seems to sink into death. He is thereby convinced that in himself, his word and his person the 'kingdom of God' has drawn near: that is, that God himself, beyond all the good and evil powers of human existence, promises to come to a man in the immediacy of victorious love and forgiveness, and that thereby arises a new and conclusively radical situation of decision for the man who hears this message.

For Christians, the encounter with Jesus means that in him we meet the man whose reality in life and death does not in any way fall short of the claim to manhood which humanity makes and which is made on humanity; that contrary to our other experiences, in this man there is a man on whom we can really rely. His disciples, whose experiences of the Good Friday catastrophe was only too real, found, as a gift of Jesus himself, that this life had not foundered, that in reality death was his *victory*, that he was accepted by the mystery of God and so became Saviour, that he 'rose again' (and by 'resurrection' I mean not a return to to this spatio-temporally and biologically composed reality which is our burden, but the definitive salvation of the whole man— 'body and soul'—in God).

Because this resurrection means being taken up by the mystery called, incomprehensibility, God, its 'how' is beyond representation. Where, however, our absolute hope and the experience of this man's life and death meet, we cannot any longer reckon with the destruction of Jesus without at the same time renouncing our own absolute hope, without falling in despair, avowedly or not, into the abyss of emptiness and ultimate nothingness. If in our own hope for ourselves we look for somewhere in man's history where we are met by one because of whom we dare to trust that here our hope is fulfilled, this search can find no namable person without the apostolic witness to Jesus.

If, however, we have encountered Jesus through that witness, then the experience of it gives us (if our hope is a free decision) the strength and courage, from within our own existence, which is hope, to say: He is risen. Man's essentially hopeful constitution and his historical experience conjoin in the Christian and become one: HE, Jesus, is the one accepted by God; the question which man is in the limitlessness of incomprehensibility is answered by God in Jesus; in Jesus humanity has successfully achieved definitive happiness, and the sceptical question about man in his uselessness and guilt is superseded. The courage of hope, which we are or can be in freedom, is sealed. HE is both *the* question and the answer (which is given in man's life) in one. HE is the ultimate, conclusive answer, because every other thinkable question is superseded by *death*, and to this all-consuming question the answer is given in him if he is the risen one. HE is *the* Word of God to us, *the* answer to the one question which we are.

In the light of this, the statements of traditional Church teaching and theology about Jesus Christ, and therefore what we mean by his 'metaphysical divine sonship', by the unity of the eternal Word of God and human reality in Jesus, make sense. But conversely what we can also say is that whoever accepts Jesus as in himself the conclusive Word of God, as the final seal on his hope, is a Christian even though he cannot, or can only with difficulty, live out these traditional formulas of Christology which arise from a particular horizon of thought not easily accessible to us today. Cross and resurrection go together in every authentic belief in Jesus.

The cross means the demand, never more to be veiled, for man's unconditional surrender to the mystery of existence which man can no longer bring under his control because he is finite and guilt-laden. Resurrection means the unconditioned hope that in that surrender man is definitively accepted by this mystery in forgiveness and blessedness, that where man lets go completely, the precipice disappears. The cross and resurrection of Jesus mean that this letting-go and not-falling because of God's activity have become, in Jesus, exemplary, and that this possibility (and also the possibility of being able to let go, which is the most difficult challenge of our lives) is irrevocably promised to us too.

Here, in Jesus, we have the actual absolute. We need only commit ourselves, lovingly and unconditionally, to this real man. Then we have everything. It is true that we must die with him. But then nobody escapes dying. Why not with him, as one with him, we say: 'My God, why have you deserted me?', and, 'Into your hands I commit my spirit'? Every metaphysics of man first becomes concrete here. And it is no longer very important how that metaphysics is or might be 'in itself'. If it is acquired in Jesus, it contains very little, and therefore everything, because it is acquired in death as life; not in speaking about death, but in death, his and one's own. In that moment, which for each individual is still to come, we have laid hold of Christianity. We may, however, prepare ourselves here and now to be open to that event. The glory of life does not vanish in it. On the contrary, everything receives its ultimate weight for the first time and yet becomes the 'light burden'. Christianity is therefore for me the simplest thing, because it signifies the one totality of existence and gives us all the ingredients as ingredients without a recipe. But the simplest thing is also the hardest. It is grace, but grace, offered to all, which can still be accepted and (as our Christian hope affirms) is still accepted even where the unconditional hope has not yet explicitly found the one it seeks as its realization: Jesus of Nazareth. Perhaps it is decreed that many 'find' him more easily when they seek him only in nameless hope, without being able to call him by his historical name. However, the man who has sufficiently clearly encountered him must confess him, because otherwise he would be denying his own hope.

If the resurrection of Jesus is the mystery's divine, victorious promise of itself to us as our definitive life, it is understandable that there would be no resurrection if Jesus did not *also* rise in our belief of his eternal validity. Hence there is a community of men who believe in him as the crucified and risen. We all find our answer in the mystery in which he is withdrawn from us, yet near to us if we face this mystery unconditionally. We call this community the Church: those who believe in Jesus cannot be merely religious individualists, because of their common relationship to the one Jesus. It therefore happens that this belief in Jesus can be passed on only through active witness, which again ultimately demands a social formation of the believing community which takes Jesus as its focal point. Christianity therefore (and for many other reasons) means Church.

Further, man is the social being who always operates the history of his ultimate freedom in and because of a socially composed community. Even the most radical religious individualist is in constant relationship to the Church through language, scripture, tradition, and so on, even though he may intend to be quite independent of it. Even truth has something to do with a public and also critical relation to society and therefore to institutions—without, of course, corrupting one's 'own' truth into pure arbitrariness (although one's 'own' truth cannot be more important to oneself if one is not to cling in arrogance and egoism to one's individual 'truth'). Individual Christian churches and confessions might not interpret the exact role of the Church in precisely the same way, but there is an institution, and so basically a desire to be the Church, in all Christian bodies. Baptism as an initiatory rite into the Christian community and confession of the three-fold God is all but universal in Christendom.

I am not saying much here on the bitter Christian question which has given rise to the most frightful events in the history of Christianity, namely whether and how the Christian conscience must make a decision of confessional significance between the various Christian denominations and churches. Up to now all Christian confessions were (basically rightly) convinced that the different creeds and the ecclesial institutions which support them were not simply merely accidental, and in the final analysis indifferent, variations of the one Christian phenomenon, but also pose a real confessional question addressed to the conscience of the individual.

Given the difficulty of historical knowledge with regard to the *exact* connexion of even the early Church with the historical Jesus, and the impossibility of any reasonably accurate interrogation of later church history for legitimate and illegitimate developments (and there have certainly been both), I myself find my relation to my Roman Catholic church in the answer to a double question: Do I find in it, without hindrance from its doctrine or an absolutely binding practice, the liberating Spirit of Jesus and his truth; and can I discover in it in historical continuity as clear and as firm a solidarity with the beginnings as possible, despite and in all the historical and indeed inevitable change? The affirmative answer to this double question seems to me to give me the right and the duty of an unconditional relationship to my church, in which, naturally, is included, of the Church's essence, a critical relationship to it as to the locus of evangelical freedom. I cannot say more here on the agonizing question of the fragmentation of the Church.

It goes without saying that every true Christian laments the social and historical shape of the Church, which in its tangible reality is bound to lag behind its essence. The Church proclaims a message which always calls its empirical reality into question. It is always the Church of sinners, whose members belie with their deeds what they confess with their lips. Frightful and mean things have blotted its history, so much so that only one consideration keeps us in it: where else could we go if we left the Church? Would we be true to the liberating Spirit of Jesus if we, who are ourselves selfish sinners, claimed to be the 'pure' by keeping this poor Church at a distance? The sole hope of doing one's bit to remedy the Church's wretchedness lies in bearing the burden of its misery, of which each member is to some extent himself guilty; in trying to live *in* the Church as a Christian, in bearing the responsibility for transforming it again and again from within (in all its confessions, it must always be the Church of the 'Reformation'). If we think we discover in ourselves some Christian feature in the true sense of the word 'Christian' and if we understand its real significance, how can we refuse to contribute it selflessly to this community of sinners who in the power of Jesus' Spirit are moving through the Church's (however wretched) history to that fulfilment which Jesus' death and resurrection promise us?

Christians have always been aware, at least in principle, that they can know, realize and prove to be credible their hoping and loving relationship to the incomprehensible mystery of their lives only in the unconditional love of their neighbour, in which alone they can really burst open the hell of their egoism. Even where it is not corrupted into a means of concealed egoism, this love for others is not by any means taken for granted; it is the liberating grace of God. Where this love is truly at work, the Spirit of Jesus is there, even when he is not named, as Matthew 25 clearly teaches us. We can only tremble and hope that somewhere in our lives the grace of God is working this wonder in us. Everything, really everything, depends on it. But it must be appreciated in an age of necessarily increasing socialization of man that such love for one's neighbour can no longer be itself if it gives shape and dignity solely to the private relationships of the individual to the individual.

Today it must be incarnated above all (if not solely) in each man's and each Christian's responsibility for the social field as such. This task is incumbent in a particular way on the individual Christian, the individual Christian group and the Church as such. The Church must make its love for others credible by its socio-political and socio-critical commitment. It has to do this by virtue of its *own* Spirit, of the Spirit of Jesus, and in the hope of eternal life. Drawing on the memory of Jesus's death and resurrection, the Church achieves a critical distance from the present state of society which allows it to absolutize neither the already acquired present nor an imminent planned future. Were the Church to become a merely 'humanitarian enterprise', it would betray its function, because it must witness to the ultimate seriousness and inconceivable dignity of this love for man in the presence of men. Yet the danger appears to be even greater today that love for one's neighbour, who today is principally secular society, is not taken seriously enough by Christians, although only in it can the God to whom, with Jesus, they wish to resign themselves totally be found —not although but *because* he is the incomprehensible mystery which not even Jesus did away with but which he in belief and hope accepted.

Christianity and the churches are slowly acquiring a new and very much more differentiated relationship to the non-Christian world religions than they had before, when those religions lay outside the circle of Christian culture. Christianity cannot, of course, renounce the claim to have heard and to preach the all-embracing and conclusive Word of Grace in Jesus the crucified and risen. But it does not deny that the Spirit of God, the Spirit in whom Jesus delivered himself up in death to God, is fulfilling a work of liberation, within human finitude and culpable wrongdoing, everywhere in history. In their own way the non-Christian world religions bear witness to this Spirit, and not only to human limitation. And many of their provisional and great experiences can be accepted as partial answers in the comprehensive answer which is Jesus, because the history of the Christian message is not yet at an end. Atheism, however, which has today become a worldwide mass phenomenon, can be understood by Christianity not only as the revelation of man's No, in which he refuses to enter into the incomprehensible mystery of God, but as a moment in the history of the experience of God in which God appears more and more radically as the adorable mystery to whom we abandon ourselves in hope.

In my life and thinking I increasingly encounter difficulties with which I 'cannot cope'. First and foremost it seems to me as if I must simply continue even though I do not know where everything ultimately leads. But I cannot help asking myself what is hidden at the bottom of this perseverance. And then I still find hope. And hope condenses the experience of life into two words: mystery and death. 'Mystery' expresses this helplessness in hope. 'Death', however, commands us not to veil this helplessness but to endure it. I look on Jesus the crucified and know that nothing will be spared me. I give myself (I hope) into his death, and hope that that joint death is the ascent of the blessed mystery. In this hope, however, life in all its beauty emerges in the darkness and everything becomes promise. I find that being a Christian is the simplest possible task, the utterly simple and therefore so difficult light burden, as the Gospel calls it. If we bear it, it bears us. The longer we live, the more difficult and the lighter it becomes.

3 The core of the faith

The world of man—not only his outer but his inner world—has, because of modern natural science, the historical sciences, the social sciences, the whole of life and thought today, become incredibly multiform. Nobody today can quite manage to harmonize and elaborate into a finished system all its manifold experiences and the conclusions of all the sciences. He knows only too well, and sees only too clearly, that there is an untold super-abundance which others know and he does not. In such a mental situation, the Christian faith at first sight looks like a small, modest body of opinion, lost in this ocean of judgments, opinions, world-views and questions, and certainly, as it would appear, no longer in a position seriously to claim to be the factor which gives order to everything in man's life and steers it to its final goal.

The apparent contingency and irrelevance of the faith in the life of modern man lose their legitimation and force, however, once we realize what exactly is believed and lived in the Christian faith.

In its real and living core, this Christian faith is not a compli-cated mass of difficult and obscure propositions the content of which is foreign to the actual experiences of our lives, but something extremely simple which once we have really grasped and experienced it cannot be separated from, or conceived apart from, our lives. This simple faith can then be broken down into a mutiplicity of single dogmas, but only if this multiplicity of doctrines is constantly referred back to, and understood to derive from, that simple living core, can the individual dogmas, in so far as they expressly engage us in our religious life as a whole (which *a priori* is not necessarily the case), become intelligible to us today.

We cannot escape the difficulty of accepting and 'realizing' this multiplicity of dogmas today just by appealing to the fact that the revelation of the dogmas was known before their content, because even the fact of this revelation cannot really be effectively substantiated today unless we also argue from the content of what is revealed. In what, then, does this simple and living core of the Christian faith, which still makes belief possible indeed easy for us today, consist?

This question can evidently be answered in a variety of ways and with a variety of different formulations, even though these various answers ultimately mean the same thing. With this reservation I shall attempt to outline a single answer here. It is in three intimately connected and mutually conditioned parts: *we who believe* know that we are ineluctably engaged by the incomprehensible mystery of our lives whom we call God, and who ceaselessly and silently grasps us and challenges our hope and love even when we show little concern for him in the practice of our lives or even actually deny him in theory; *we who believe* are convinced that this incomprehensible mystery whom we call God has definitively and forgivingly promised himself to us in the life, death and eternal living presence of Jesus of Nazareth, as the content and eternal validity of our own lives, which do not perish. *We who believe* constitute, in this confession of God in Jesus Christ, the community of believers, the Church, which attests this message of God in Jesus Christ to the whole world for its salvation. I shall pause a little at each of the three fundamental statements of the faith so that we can appreciate more easily that our faith still meets the needs of our human situation today and is still credible.

1 THE COMPREHENSIVE GROUND

Our existence is embraced by an ineffable mystery whom we call God. We can exclude him from our day-to-day awareness by the concerns and activity of our daily lives; we can drown the all-pervading silence of this mystery. But he is there: as the one comprehensive, all-bearing ground of all reality; as the comprehensive question that remains when all individual answers have been given; as the goal to which we reach beyond all individual goals and all individual good things of life; as the future which lies beyond all individual goals and keeps our ceaseless restless striving in motion; as the ultimate guarantee that there is really a responsibility for our freedom which cannot be shifted on to someone else, which we cannot elude by leaping into nothingness; as the one truth in which all individual knowledge has its ultimate home and order; as the promise that selfless love will not be disappointed.

This ultimate mystery at the root of reality and of our lives is nameless, impenetrable, something we cannot dominate with our concepts and life calculations, something that gives itself only when we yield to it in worship. We call it God. But this 'name' is only a reminder of the nameless and the incomprehensible, of the bright abyss to which our life tends, either to perish in it for ever or to find its definitive fulfilment. Every science, even the most up-to-date and advanced, deals with individual things and establishes connexions among them in order to be able to control them in the service of life. No science, however, can dominate the one mystery which embraces everything and which in all partial knowledge becomes only the more incomprehensible and burning; either all sciences flee it in doubt and confusion, or they must rise in man to the worship of the fundamental mystery of all reality and all life.

When the sciences reach their limits (which can be experienced even when an unlimited land of investigable matter still lies stretched out before them), either they leave man resigned, alone with his question about the unity and totality of his world and reality, or they try—and in the end fatally—to explain the ultimate questions away as meaningless and unanswerable, or they appeal in sceptical despair to nothingness, which contains no answer. We who believe, however, do not flee this ultimate mystery, we enter into it, we know that this abyss is the only ground on which in the final analysis we can build. We appeal to this mystery; we make it the centre of our lives, the goal to which all the roads of our history lead, even though and precisely because they lead into the incomprehensible.

We call this mystery God, and when we confess our belief in God, we know that in our lives, at the heart of our lives, we have to do business with this God, to experience always the inexpressibility of his mystery, because we are always the questioners who can never definitively arrive there, because we are and remain in everything in our lives, right up to the last question which is death, the ones about whom we are asking questions.

2 PROMISED IN THE MAN JESUS

This one great, and on our own strength unanswerable, question about this mystery called God now becomes: How does this incomprehensible mystery of our lives relate to us? Does it remain the eternally unattainable distance? the question which can be answered only from within itself but which in fact keeps silent? Is this mystery the frightful judgment on the guilt which our lives can conceal in their empty depths? Or will this distance approach us, give itself to us as the mystery laden with blessedness? Can the infinite, infinitely distant future become our present? Can the abyss become a saving and salvific refuge, our definitive home? Is there a forgiveness which can cancel even a guilt so far gone that it lacks the inner ability to overcome itself?

A Christian constantly feels in himself as a man the huge courage (at least as possibility and offer) to pledge himself that this mystery called God is in reality and remains not far distant; that it is not merely a judgment on our finitude and guilt, but gives itself in its own ungraspable infinity to life, truth and love. We Christians call this God-borne courage, 'technically', the Holy Spirit: the grace of faith, hope and love. And we are convinced that because of God's will with regard to *all* men this courage is offered to *all* men as the highest possibility so that they may accept it. Indeed we hope, without drawing a definite, clear-cut line, that *all* men actually accept this courage somewhere and at some time in their lives, although we cannot theorize on this hope to the point of affirming the definite salvation of all.

A Christian, however, in his faith, is also convinced that this question which the mystery poses and thereby calls all of us into question can be answered ultimately and certainly and historically only by one man, of whom we can confidently believe that he is, in his life and death as man, both a question and God's answer to that question in one, through Jesus of Nazareth. We know him through the Gospels and the message of Christianity. We know about his life, which was as ours are, full of effort and misery; we know the depth of his love for the incomprehensible God, whom he called his Father, and for men, whom he loved unconditionally although they hated him. We know about his trust in God and men, the incomprehensible darkness of his death. We know in the faith of Christianity which has not foundered after two thousand years that precisely in his collapse into the abyss of a Godforsaken death he could save his life in God, that he conquered in his failure, and found both himself and the incomprehensibility of God as blessed life. This victory through death, this definitive ascent through ruin we call his resurrection and his ascension to the Father's right hand. We look on his life and death, and his Spirit grants us the confidence—which gives us hope for ourselves and which we call the Christian faith—that this life with its love, its obedience and its loyalty was not lost but is eternally saved.

So for us this Jesus is God's answer to the one comprehensive question which we ourselves are and which we are posed. In belief in him as God's ultimate definitive answer to us we are confident that the mystery we call God will, in forgiveness and final blessed-

ness, communicate himself to us in that which we call the Holy
Spirit of God and, in that Spirit's definitive overshadowing of us,
eternal life. Why should we not believe in this Jesus as in God's
definite promise of himself? Is there, among the great spirits of
humanity, the sages and the prophets, one on whom one would
rather rely and to whom one would rather entrust oneself with
one's questionable life? Or have we, who are a radical question
about how the eternal mystery of our existence wishes to relate to
us, the right to waive an ultimate answer when this answer (which
we certainly cannot force) is offered to us and accepted by countless men in faith, hope and love as the true and ultimate answer
of life?

We believe in Jesus the Christ, that is, in God's self-promise in
forgiveness and eternal life which has been persuasively announced in his life. No one forces us to accept in faith God's
answer, who is Jesus crucified and risen. But also no one can
convince us that there is another, better and more comprehensive
answer to the question ineluctably and inexorably posed by our
own life, even when we try to ignore this question. No one will
persuade us that we have not heard the question. Once we pose it
and face up to it, we find it easy to believe that in Jesus we have
heard an answer to it.

This answer does not answer all the thousand and one questions of a particular kind which our life poses, but it contains all
these individual answered or unanswered questions in the saving
mystery of God. All these questions of life ultimately come together in the one question which death poses in our life. But we
have the courage of believing hope to fall with Jesus' death into
the abyss of God as into our own definitiveness, our home and our
eternal life. Because we can confidently die only with him, and
because we still die with him when, even without knowing him
explicitly, we surrender in calm hope to the mystery of life, we
can here and now live this life in confidence with him even
though it still stands under the mystery of death.

3 LIVED IN THE COMMUNITY OF FAITH

It is but a short step from here to the third part of my reflexions,
the Church. Because it is addressed to all mankind as a unity,
God's answer to us in Jesus Christ is not a purely private matter
for individuals. It creates a community of faith and confession; it
brings a Church into being. We are the community of faith in
God in Jesus Christ. We confess him as God's answer to man and
as man's answer to God, as the unity of man's question, God's
answer to humanity and man's reply to this answer in Jesus the

author of faith. We are the believers in God and Jesus Christ in brotherly communion, and consequently we are the Church. We experience this faith as our redeemed freedom and as a mission to the world, which by means of this faith throughout its entire history is to find God as its definitive goal.

Naturally this community of belief, called the Church, elaborates its social structures, its officials, its changing history all too often laden with human narrowness, guilt and disunion, on the pattern of the needs of human association, according to God's and Jesus' will. However, the person who really knows what this community of belief is ultimately concerned with, namely God in Jesus Christ, can endure this believing communion with calm patience—even though it is composed of poor men who, also as Church, are on their way from guilt to forgiveness—knowing as he does that he contributes his own narrowness and guilt to this community which is centred on and borne up by Christ. For him the scandal of the Church, however great, is not greater and more intolerable than the scandal of the guilt, chaos and narrowness of human history.

He ranges himself humbly in the community of these believers which is on pilgrimage through the darkness of the world to eternal light. He knows he is near God when with fraternal patience, readiness to forgive and in hope he is and remains near men, and so also near the men of the Church.

At its deepest level our Christian faith is simple, living, inexhaustible and, because it concerns man's ultimate destiny, valid and effective for today and for tomorrow. We can still confidently believe today if our spirit and our heart have really found this inmost centre of the Christian faith.

We may still notice that many individual developments of this simple faith in the almost incalculable mass of individual doctrines remain alien and well-nigh unintelligible. We can, however, confidently and humbly let them rest, trusting that our own understanding of the faith will grow and mature into a closer and closer assimilation to the belief of the Church in all times and cultures. We can still believe as Christians and Catholics today, even though we know that our own faith is still on the way and as long as we do not turn our momentary understanding into the definitive norm of faith.

4 What is truth?

When we read some 'stories', we cannot help asking whether what is related is an 'actual historical event', in the usual sense of that phrase. With relation to Pilate's question in John 18 : 38a, however, such a question seems unimportant from the first, because the real 'truth' of this dialogue between Jesus and Pilate and so of Pilate's question in particular will in any case be apparent to the reader if he reads the passage with attention and an open mind, and in the context of the whole Gospel: the reality and life-and-death importance of an encounter between God (in Jesus) and a man.

It seems to me that this exchange between Jesus and Pilate belongs to a series of 'encounters' which runs through the whole of John's Gospel. As a general theme, this series of life-and-death encounters is announced in John 1 : 9–12, and then we have successively Jesus' meetings with: the two disciples (1 : 37 ff.), Peter (1 : 41 f.), Philip (1 : 43), Nathaniel (1 : 47–50), Nicodemus (John 3, where Nicodemus' ultimate reaction remains obscure; but cf. 7 : 50 ff.; 19 : 39), the Samaritan woman at Jacob's well (4 : 7–29), the court official (4 : 46–53), the thirty-eight-year-old invalid (5 : 5–9, 14 ff.), the Twelve (6 : 67–71), the adulterous woman (8 : 9–11), the man born blind (9 : 35–8), Martha (11 : 20–7), Pilate (18 : 33–8), Mary Magdalene after the resurrection (20 : 14–17), Thomas (20 : 26–9), and finally Peter (21 : 15–19). These 'encounters' should not be stylized (as part of form criticism, or in some other way) into their own literary genre. They are too self-evident for that and too different in their situations, in their particular details (as opposed to the many other conversations of Jesus in John and the other Gospels) and above all in their outcomes. All these accounts, however, are of life-and-death meetings of individuals with Jesus in which the dialogue is not ultimately concerned with some third factor accessible outside and in the final analysis existing independently of this dialogue, but in which the relationship of the two partners—one of whom is Jesus as he reveals himself in John: the Way, the Truth and the Life (John 14:6)—is itself the dialogue. When we view Pilate's question in the context of this series of encounters and consider that it does not always have to have a salvific outcome (John 1:11), the importance of the exchange between Jesus and Pilate and therefore also of Pilate's question becomes clearer.

Of the meeting between Jesus and Pilate I shall consider here only Pilate's question. It does not prejudice these reflexions if I presume and state that Pilate has not discerned and grasped, and concretely could not discern and grasp, the actual Jesus as whom Jesus reveals himself to Pilate in this dialogue; because precisely on this presumption the encounter means that one can also ignore Jesus, to one's unsalvation, even when one can claim, as a matter of daily fact, that one could not recognize Jesus and therefore did not in fact reject him (cf. for example Matthew 25:44 f.).

It could be said that the point (as Pilate intended it) of his sceptical question was the expression of his conviction that a question about 'truth' has nothing to do with realistic and pragmatic politics in which alone, in this situation, he is interested and needs to be interested, and that therefore one who is in the service of this truth and occupies himself with nothing else is from the first indifferent to him. Already on the basis of this 'conviction' Pilate found Jesus guiltless. Procurators are seldom philosophers (as Schlier rightly points out), and so Pilate's question (which is in effect a rejection) primarily means only that he wishes to remain at the level of his competence, and therefore of politics, and that in politics one does not advance with questions about truth; that there is no politically relevant truth, and therefore no 'political theology' either. Curiously, there are Christians who justify withdrawal into the sacristy and non-Christians who justify their censure of the sacristy with the very same arguments, and it seems to be ultimately indifferent whether 'truth', thus rated as unimportant for the reality of the earth, does not actually exist at all or exists only in heaven.

But whatever the intended point of Pilate's sceptical question, for which Pilate does not apologize (an omission the more heinous in that his 'theoretical' neutrality then leads him to the condemnation of the guiltless Jesus and so to a political outrage), it must be said that 'Pilate, faced with the truth, avoids it because he knows and acknowledges no truth' (Schlier); he wishes to be neutral in questions of truth. This, however, is impossible. At least subconsciously it also signifies a radical opposition to Jesus and leads him unresistingly to the disaster which precisely he was trying to avoid by maintaining his neutrality. It is therefore indifferent what undertones one detects in this question: a thirst for knowledge, arrogance, scorn, or the bitterest despair of the sceptic.

In the Old and New Testaments and in subsequent church and salvation history, there are many 'key concepts'—some of them superseded by others—in which man, depending throughout on his particular actual historical situation is confronted with the ultimate mystery of the one totality of his existence and with the absolute mystery (called God) who incomprehensively embraces and permeates him: for example, law (in the positive, salvific and redemptive sense of the Old Testament), light, life, Logos, spirit, freedom, love. In these reference is mare from a certain historically specific situation and experience to the mystery of God addressing us. Johannine 'truth' belongs to these key concepts. Not only 'truth', however. And not only in John.

We ourselves are asked in Pilate's question under what key concept we are in danger, in our own collective and individual situation, of shutting our minds off in despairing scepticism from this salvation-bearing mystery of our existence. This No in our lives does not need an explicit question like Pilate's before it is affirmed; it can emerge from the activity of life refusing to clarify and explicitate its own significance. For example, one can ask, from within and by means of the dailiness of one's life, the sceptical question: What is love, or responsibility, or loyalty, or hope? and so on.

All these sceptically negative questions are, as I pointed out for Pilate's, a rejection of Jesus of Nazareth, whether we expressly know it or not, because he is the mysterious universal actuality whom we meet incognito wherever the content of these key concepts comes to challenge us and forces us to step outside the circle we had, in our attempt at autonomy, marked out as the radius of our lives. We are each one of us asked how we are in danger of formulating our own Pilate's question, how we shall try to exclude from our concrete and particular life-circle the call of God and of Jesus.

5 What is evangelization?

If my calculations are correct, the words '*evangelizatio*' and '*evangelizare*' occur forty times in the documents of Vatican II. It is therefore a current concept in the council's terminology. In general, 'evangelize', 'evangelization' are words seldom used in Catholic theology. In the Evangelical or Protestant Church of Germany, for example, the word 'evangelization' occurs frequently. It is (or was) used for the winning over of non-evangelical Christians to the evangelical churches as well as for the efforts of the numerous and varied 'revivalist' movements to animate life in the churches.

I can say here only what *I* should like to understand by the word 'evangelization' or what *I* should especially emphasize in such a concept today. 'Evangelization' means for me simply the ever new proclamation of the Gospel of Jesus crucified and risen as the pledge that God communicates *himself* in forgiveness and 'divinization' in his Spirit (as himself the strength of the way and the goal of life) and in so doing shapes the ultimate unity of men among themselves and of their history until what already *is* stands fully revealed: that God is all in all and the inmost centre (in grace) of our existence in the loving and hoping community of men. Such 'evangelization' is addressed to all men, is therefore on the one hand 'mission' in the usual sense of that term, but on the other an ever new proclamation of the Gospel to Christians because they are always on the way to becoming Christians in the ever new situations of their lives and of their society. 'Evangelization' should be not *merely* an 'indoctrination' from without, but (depending on the present situation of the proclaimer and his hearer) an initiation.

That is to say that the proclamation echoes the questions which the hearer is asking; it can also, of course, stimulate questions which the hearer has brushed aside or not sufficiently explicitated in his consciousness, and in particular it calls up the ultimate and comprehensive questions, therefore also those questions which the man in the street today has rejected and excluded from his consciousness. Such an initiation as this proceeds from the Christian conviction that *prior to* all proclamation God is already and always, in the offer of his self-communication in the Holy Spirit, in man as *the* question and *the* answer (in one), even when they remain unspoken, and that therefore the proclamation of the Gospel tells man only what he already *is* (at least in the sense of a really offered possibility): the one freely given God's incomprehensibility, into which, in the course of his life, he lets himself go in freedom, hope and love (unless he opposes the ultimate meaning of his own freedom with a No). As initiation, 'evangelization' borders closely on meditation and prayer. Where it is no more than authoritarian indoctrination, it fails in its purpose. As a call to the inmost centre of pardoned man, it is also a 'morality', but it does not 'moralize'.

Correctly understood, this initiation is, certainly, a call to man's innermost centre of existence, but it is not a call to man in individualistic 'solitude' even though it must teach a man to entrust his permanent solitude to God. It appeals to the community of those who assemble round Jesus in faith, hope and love; it appeals to the Church because it is the confession that the *one* Spirit of the living God is for all; it must proclaim that we can never fulfil the responsibility of our own freedom to the mystery of God within our own existence apart from our neighbour (in every sense of that word). It is what true Christian love for both God and man together means, and that is the way in which man becomes really free with regard to all permanent inner and outer pressures; we are free if we help to 'free' our neighbour (the struggle for more 'emancipation' is also, but not solely, germane here).

Evangelization presumes a community (and therefore the unity of communities: the Church) as a witness to the effectiveness of the proclamation, and creates a community in which fraternal love is exercised without the preaching of the Word of God becoming merely the kind of shrill little bell we so often hear today.

2
PRACTICE

1 The sword of faith

We celebrate the memory of the death of Jesus, our Lord, as his return to the mystery which God is, and as the event which means for us in our history the promise that our life and our death are safe for ever in the love of God. We celebrate this *memoria Christi* on the day on which we think about his presentation in the temple, when his mother, in unconditional faith, put her infant son at God's service.

That feast of the presentation directs our thoughts to the figure of the Blessed Virgin as described in Luke's pericope on the presentation in the temple (2: 22–35). The figure is that of the believer. Simeon makes a twofold statement about Mary: that this ultimate event in the history of belief which her child is is a sign that is rejected, destined for the fall and for the rising of many, and that such a happening will pierce her *own* existence, *her* heart and in her the heart of *every* believer, like a two-edged sword.

That is the effect of faith. Faith is a sword which pierces and divides. In Matthew 10: 34 Jesus himself says that he has come to bring not peace but a sword. Faith is suffering the torment of this sword, the refusal therefore to presume too rashly that we are reconciled, the readiness to live in hope, at the depths of oneself, with the conflict that brings disunity and fragmentation into our existence, and this to the point at which only one course can be chosen: despair or unconditional surrender to that mysterious unity and reconciliation whom we call God. Faith is peace, freedom, trust, joy and much else besides. But it is also this: suffering the torment of the sword at the heart of our existence. This sword of disunion in the whole of life affects everyone, whether he wishes it or not. Belief in the Word who reveals himself to us for our sake does not allow us to ignore this impassable disunity, and calls us to accept it, endure it, carry it through life in hope. Naturally such lifelong acceptance is possible only when we labour to reconcile these inreconciled realities, to integrate what is plural, because otherwise what we would really be trying to do would be to deny or neutralize the sword in our existence.

It would therefore be unbelief if we tried with eudemonist or stoical intent to hasten and force the reconciled integration of our lives in our private existence, instead of patiently and confidently enduring the changing, the unpredictable, the contradictory and the unforeseeable, and renouncing all desire to cook our history up by our own recipes.

It would be unbelief if we thought we could live in the social dimension by means of a ready-made ideology, whatever it might be, which would make us the absolutely sovereign planners of our future, instead of being (weary but hopeful) pilgrims constantly searching for the way to the absolute future so that then, when we have found it, we can appropriate it to ourselves in grace and undeservedly.

It would be unbelief if we thought we had in science and the sciences a system into which we could autarchically integrate all our partial perceptions—which are precisely *not* integrated—in enjoyed harmony. It would be unbelief to suppose with a little philosophical or theological talk or with the monomania of a particular science which aspires to universality that we could heal the pain of knowing that every progress of knowledge, in whatever area, increasingly confronts the individual with what he does not know and does not control, and once did not know that he did not know, while true theology is precisely reflexion on the fact that there is only one who reconciles truths, who integrates them into his one truth: God, who has promised us that *his* truth will one day be our happiness.

It would be unbelief if we did not wish to speak with praise and worship of him whom we cannot dominate in our scientific systems, if we wished to speak only of what is clear, that is, of what confirms our thought in its authority instead of overwhelming it.

It is faith, on the other hand, if we accept the thrust of the sword in our existence: the sword of the question which has no answer, the sword that all life in its pain ends in death, the sword that love does not resolve all contradictions in this life, the sword that every goal reached becomes a beginning again, the sword of farewell, of disappointment, of growing old, of our own stupidities, both culpable and inculpably naïve, the sword of the bitter things which heralds the approach of death.

This sevenfold sword pierces our existence, and then our transfixed heart is open to the promise which is the nameless God himself. According to the Book of Revelation (1:16), the two-edged sword issues from the mouth of the Son of Man, who was himself transfixed as he hung on the cross (John 19: 34; cf. Revelation 1: 7). If he is the one who was pierced, our faith in him can be nowhere else but in suffering the torment of the sword which strikes through our existence. When we speak of faith, we speak also (not only) of hope in surrender and surrender in hope. The person who takes this to be an elegant stroke of dialectics has not understood. He should be referred to where in his past or future life he meets with impasses which leave him dumbfounded and despairing. There—where the fight for earthly justice brings forth injustice, where love is betrayed and little children, the innocents, die, where noble minds decay, where men treat men worse than wolves, and so forth—he could learn what is meant here. Should we perhaps not say such things when we celebrate the Lord's death? It is the proper time, though, surely.

And if there is someone who thinks of life more serenely, accepts life more cheerfully, life will be given him, provided that he acknowledges this great courage and this joy as grace which promises the believer that eternal reconciliation is still on its way, and we therefore proclaim the Lord's death until he comes.

If the dead live, if the departed are not those whose life has melted into the void but rather those whose history has found its finality in God, we have the right and the sacred duty again and again to confess the validity of their lives, the lives of all those who have preceded us in the sign of faith. In this we also confess her whose soul the sword of pain pierced, who again according to Luke was blessed because she believed (Luke 1: 45). When we confess the law of her life, the law of her faith, we are calling on her, and we are paying her homage as the model of all believers.

We celebrate the memory of the Lord's death. We thereby confess that we do not wish to accept the sword of our existence, wherever and in whatever form it comes, as if we had no hope. We celebrate the Lord's death in worship and festival so that we can celebrate it in the blessed bitterness of life, in us, around us and also in our knowing, which cannot be perfected this side of death. Let us proclaim the Lord's death until he comes.

2 The possibility and necessity of prayer

The question I am trying to answer here is as follows: is it possible to pray today? A second question—*what form* prayer must take today if it is to be meaningful—is not really another, second question, because it too expresses, although in another grammatical form, the one, unique and entire situation of modern man: Is it possible to pray today?

1. PRELIMINARIES

What has just been said applies equally to the preliminaries of the question: the following three remarks, rightly viewed, are not to be taken as dealing with the main body of the question of prayer, but are rather to be understood as a sort of preparation for the great theme, 'prayer'.

(a) Praying as a fundamental act of human existence

There are realities in human life which, because they concern and actualize the whole man, cannot be constructed and understood from a point outside themselves. There is no extrinsic point for the realization of the whole man from which this realization could be determined and constructed as by an independent system of coordination in such a way that it could be understood before it happened. The reality of love, loyalty, trust, hope, anguish and so on can be grasped in its potentiality and significance only in the actual performance of such fundamental events of human existence. These events cannot and could not be properly investigated synthetically from without. If they apparently are, they have fallen short of their real essence. One can discover and talk about events like these only as already occurring realities, and then either accept them as offers to one's freedom or brush them aside and let them die. This is true of prayer, because if it exists at all and is to have a meaning, prayer is just such a total, fundamental act of human existence embracing that existence as a whole and bringing it, in a movement of trust and love, to that mystery whom we call God.

Prayer too, then, can be grasped as possible and meaningful only in its execution. It too must be experienced as something that in a true sense has already been given to us; only thus can it be accepted (or by the same token thrust aside and condemned to extinction). We can never speak about prayer, then, unless we include some reference to the fact that it has already been given to us in the depths of our existence, to the fact of this hidden entreaty of the Spirit of God, as Paul calls it, to which we must join our own voices in the activity of our freedom.

In earlier times, when God was a self-evident reality in the public consciousness of society, it was easy to explain what prayer meant and consequently easy to bring man to an appreciation of its essence and necessity almost rationally, as if one were approaching prayer from some extrinsic standpoint. Today, however, when, despite our faith, which we have and of course defend, we find ourselves asking, with what sometimes amounts to anguish, what exactly is meant by this word God, where this God, whose presence in a world interpreted by the exact sciences with their methodical atheism is not exactly self-evident, is in fact to be found, then prayer (in the widest sense of that word) becomes itself the place in which we meet God; God has ceased to be the self-evident point of departure which would make the essence and necessity of prayer intelligible as it were extrinsically. Prayer—and in prayer God—must be its own justification and its own advertisement.

(b) Praying as an historical constant of humanity

There is a history of prayer, and it is coextensive with the history of man. This prayer might (in the course of man's history) take on the strangest forms, might go radically astray relative to its content and its addressee. But in all its contortions and historical forms, it always appears as that mysterious procedure by which a person lets himself go into the ultimate mystery of his existence as such, trustingly, explicitly, thematically. It is so, however: prayer is universal in the history of mankind. This should at least give us food for thought when we ask whether prayer is still possible *today*. Of course a lot has become possible and a lot impossible. We may therefore ask whether we should still pray for protection from lightning when we feel more secure under a lightning conductor.

The history of prayer should make us wary, however, when we notice that as far as the original, fundamental realization of human existence is concerned, man has not at all or hardly at all changed in comparison with earlier times, that love, loyalty, existential anguish, disillusionment, jealousy, awareness of responsibility and so on rule men's lives today as in the past and only their empirical objective mediation has changed; when we consider further that prayer—if we can actually give this word a meaning and must do even when we reject it—is still part of this basic realization which has not really changed through the modern times of rationalism; when finally we observe that all such fundamental realities, and not only prayer, are the objects of frequent, sceptical doubt, are subject to attempts at solution and further explanation and yet remain and are still experienced as much and as persistently as before. Then the history of prayer, which is as long as the history of man, should at least make us wary of the suggestion that prayer is something which, like magic, for example, maledictory practices or conjurations, belongs to archaic times and is today nothing but a sad relic and sediment from the past, which persists because modern man's existence is still rationally underenlightened.

(c) Praying and the exact sciences

This third preliminary remark is closely connected with the first. Man would become schizophrenic in an existential (even if not necessarily psychiatric) sense if he were to accept impartially and trustfully in his life only what he had filtered through the so-called exact sciences and *thereby* proved to himself as valid, and if he were to consider as real and important only what he had retained of his life by this method. However much, in many respects, man is also the object of exact natural sciences (among which we may number empirical psychology and similar disciplines), he is as little adequately determinable by such sciences, simply because the thinking behind, and free execution of, all these sciences cannot themselves be known in the same methodical way as the realities which are extrinsic to this thinking and this freedom, or in the same way as the events that take place exclusively within human experience.

The horizons and conditions of possibility of all particular and functionally thinking sciences can be reflected on to some extent, and man always knows in a formal anticipation not only what is thought and known but also the thinking itself and its totality.

However, thinking and freedom cannot be thought of in the same way as the objective content of thought and the freely performed objective action.

It follows that the (as we may call it transcendental) experience is always and unquestionably bigger than that which the exact sciences can objectify when they establish objective and functional connexions. However, because it cannot in the last analysis ever be eliminated, this 'more' is not the regrettable remnant of the not-yet-known which persists in the exact sciences for all their strivings, but that which in life is experienced, accepted or rejected as mystery and must be grasped and expressed with quite a different form of reflexion than can be the case with the exact sciences: namely in ontological, moral and religious statements and ways of knowledge.

Even when in his sceptical science Jacques Monod leaves the ultimate particles of his biochemistry and genetics to chance and necessity, *he* bears responsibility, loves, and so on in his life; what happens then is simply not the same as, cannot be reduced to, what happens in his science. Because man today is slowly acquiring the possibility of understanding and controlling himself like a grandiose computer, he is horribly tempted to understand himself *only* as a computer. However, not the most gigantic computer with all the self-regulating mechanisms ever invented built into it can be thought of as self-given, as a total question to itself, as given over to itself in freedom. Even the biggest computer is indifferent both to itself as a totality (as opposed to single moments) and to those who maintain and balance the whole system. That does not alter the fact that today we are beginning to notice vastly more clearly how much there is about man and his consciousness that can and must be understood from a primarily technological and cybernetic point of view, unlike his own self-givenness-as-subject and his self-awareness.

I may be permitted here a brief observation on this attempt at self-destruction (which can never in fact be successful) which can make man schizophrenic through the tyranny of an exact science and rob him of confidence in that which these sciences sift out but which is still to be found in life. Prayer is precisely the or one realization of the one, single subject as such, which can never be the object of the exact sciences. Where modern man treats prayer with typical modern mistrust, that grandiosely horrific judgment, that only the objects of those functional sciences are the true and reliable reality on which man can seriously build, while everything else which escapes such exact and lucid treatment belongs to the realm of dreams and optional opinions which one is best to leave alone or suppress—until, of course, these suppressed realities make a savage comeback in a wild irrationalism of emotion and social aggression—is, expressly or secretly, at work.

2. MODERN MAN'S QUESTIONS BEFORE PRAYER

When we come to examine the basic difficulties which to modern man seem to make prayer hard or impossible, we can usefully reduce them to three: the fact that belief in God is itself threatened; the difficulty of understanding God as a 'person' who can meaningfully address man in prayer; and the particular difficulty of petitionary prayer (which is the predominant form of prayer) in view of the apparent necessity and immutability of the world's course and the insignificance before God of what we usually pray for.

(a) Threatened belief

It is evident that we cannot here properly, expressly and in detail go into the first difficulty of prayer, which is prompted by the apparent absence and intangibility of God and by modern atheism in all its different shapes and forms. It is far beyond the possibility of a short reflexion devoted specifically to prayer to treat of the question of God, although it is fundamental to the possibility and meaningfulness of prayer.

When and where a person accepts himself in the totality of his existence and so experiences himself as one confronted with the incomprehensible mystery embracing his existence and letting him submerge himself more and more deeply in this mystery in knowledge and freedom, he is living out what prayer really is and means, and he experiences what is meant by God and the ground of all reality and all self-reflexion in personhood.

Prayer is the event of the experience of God himself (in the original and all-bearing sense of experience). The question of God and the question of prayer are not properly two questions that must and can be answered consecutively, but *one* question, even though it can be articulated as two, namely, as the question of what prayer is in its personal source in an individual, and the question of what exactly the beyond is to which prayer in its infinite extent and comprehensiveness is directed, and which is called God, who is given in prayer as a ray of hope and love shining out into infinity.

(b) The mystery of God

There are certainly many people today who find prayer difficult even though they are prepared to confess the unnameable, nameless God as the one ground of all, as the all-permeating mystery.

They are under the impression that because this nameless God is an as it were faceless and ineffable mystery he cannot be addressed. They think, more or less explicitly and reflexively, that he who bears and embraces all should not be turned by prayer into an 'object' of thought and speech, addressed and separated from all he bears.

Because he can be correctly thought of only when he is strictly understood as the all-overwhelming and incomprehensible mystery, these people think one cannot name him without turning him into an idol. They think they may not reach out in prayer to one who has no name, who as mystery cannot be 'clearly' expressed. They prefer to keep silent with averted face before this God and resignedly make for those regions of existence in which lie before one's mind and heart the individual surveyable realities with which one can really deal knowing what one is about and what is to be expected.

There is much to be commended in these sentiments. Prayer can be itself only when it is understood as the last moment of speech before the silence, as the act of self-disposal just before the incomprehensibility of God disposes of one, as the reflexion immediately preceding the act of letting oneself fall, after the last of one's own efforts and full of trust, into the infinite Whole which reflexion can never grasp.

Accepting all this, however, we have also to say that we can and must undertake the ever new venture of addressing this incomprehensible God. Such address does not, of course, take place, as in the interhuman field, on a horizon which supports the exchange and embraces both partners of the dialogue like a third party. *God* is the very possibility of address, he himself brings our prayer about when we pray. But if this is so, he can also be the one addressed. Here we need not raise the question—which we can leave to Christian philosophers and theologians—whether such a possibility of a real address to God, in which although himself the ground of speech God is yet the one spoken to, belongs to man's essence or is made possible only by what in Christian terminology we should call God's self-communication in grace, or Holy Spirit.

We can also leave open the question whether prayer as an address to God is possible only because in his self-communication to the world, called grace or Spirit, God not only carries history but made history his own and gave himself as a partner in it when, in a truly historical revelation, he addressed us in the world with the word which the world is. And the question is also open as to what and how far the rendering possible and meaningfulness of our prayer has to do with Jesus of Nazareth and his prayer to the Father, however important it is for our prayer in the concrete.

Whatever the answers to these subtler questions, man can at all events speak to God, address him and in his address come to him —if he is really praying, that is, and not attempting to subject God to himself with some form of conjuration—in grace as the place of prayer, which is everywhere. It is not easy to render this statement intelligible, because it is the very loftiest thing one can say about man. That the creature can 'treat' with his creator, that is, that the creature, radically dependent and caused as he is, the one who in his very being is derived, by turning back on himself; to some extent can 'do business' with his Ground, and in that 'business' must still know and realize that what he is doing is God's work to the very last, is certainly a statement which finally establishes, in a still more comprehensive theological proposition, that, precisely because of and not merely despite his radical dependence on God, the creature is a genuine, true reality who does not evaporate into essencelessness when he faces God, that God can in sober reality create a free other to stand before him and relate to him.

A product of man's hands does not talk to its creator. God, however, can in his all-powerfulness so posit us that we are really something in his sight and with relation to him. Here dependence and autonomy are two qualities which increase in equal and not inverse proportion. This basic relationship between God and the creature, as Christians understand it, must be clear if we are to understand the possibility of a prayerful address of the creature to God.

All this, however, is only by way of introduction. I must return to something I was saying earlier in my preliminary remarks: prayer exists, and in it God becomes our You, the one addressed of whom we have a fundamental expectation that he can answer, that he has addressed his word to us even before we begin to speak, that our address to God is therefore an answering address. Prayer like this exists. And all questions about the legitimation of prayer as an address to God must start from this fact. The axiom that it is legitimate to argue from reality to possibility is particularly pertinent here.

We pray, mankind prays, therefore we *can* say You to God. We do not need first to devise some essence for man and then, basing ourselves on that pregiven and predevised essence, inquire into whether such an essence can meaningfully address its own incomprehensible, unearthly ground and abyss. We start from the reality of such worshipping address and must then determine man's essence in basing ourselves on that reality: man is the one who can say You to God; his finitude and his dependence are such that they are open in autonomy to God as his partner, to whom of course man in prayer must still surrender as the one who has received everything, including the ability to address God and the address itself, from the one he addresses.

Therefore one must venture and not tire of venturing to speak to this You; ignoring the paradox of it, one must struggle for and suffer a higher naïvety, as the first and provisional naïvety, which conceived of self and God too ingenuously as two realities who could establish a mutual relationship, is as it were shrivelled up in the mortal terror at God's incomprehensibility and all-bearing power. When this ability to say You to God is no longer self-evident but experienced as man's highest possibility, given and disclosed by God, when we notice that the word we speak to God in such a way that it can really reach him is worked and spoken by him in us, when (to adopt the sublime language of New Testament theology) we experience that God's Spirit must pray in us and he himself say Abba, Father as our word if we are to be able to say Father, then our address to God has for the first time found its true essence, has not become impossible, as we might think, but on the contrary has for the first time become what it must be.

When we step outside the circle in which we utter this You in prayer, the possibility of prayer as an address to God films over to the point of disappearing from view. God then becomes a faceless entity, the obscure mystery who almost threatens to rebuff us, who reveals the full extent of our nothingness, and faced with whom the words stick in our throat.

If, however, we find the sudden courage still to speak our You into this darkness in hope and trust, if we do this again and again, if we make no arrogant demand that our call into this silent darkness should receive an immediate, particular answer which simply overwhelms us instead of being the soft and silently saving presence of this mystery, we notice that we can say You to God, trusting and so waiting for the moment when this mystery of our existence will show his face unveiled as everlasting love, which is an eternal You to You.

(c) The permanent function of petition

I come finally to the third difficulty man experiences with prayer today: the question of petitionary prayer. There is a tendency in modern theology to ease this difficulty by seeing prayer in terms solely of doxology, praise, confession, adoration, honour with regard to God, before whom all petition wholly retires. It is no doubt self-evident, or should be, that petition as merely making known in demand or in appeal to condescension and compliance one's own will is not in itself prayer. We must therefore try and view the matter from a different angle.

Attempts have been made to facilitate an apologia for prayer of petition by saying that one can or should in genuine petitionary *prayer* ask for only 'heavenly' things, not earthly things for the satisfaction of needs immersed in the dailiness of life, because, it is said, such earthly things are to be conquered by the struggle of our own efforts: to expect them from God without our own exertions is simply to ask God for marvels, for miraculous interventions in the world's course which do not exist, cannot exist or are reserved for God's very special friends, among whom we should not be too ready to number ourselves.

There is much in all this that is true and to be borne in mind if we are to maintain a clear distinction between the essence of prayer and magical conjuration. However, we should not be in too much of a hurry to try to sublimate and 'demythologize' petitionary prayer, because throughout the history of religion men have resorted to genuine and (if one may so call it) 'solid' prayer of petition.

The Old Testament Psalms, which Christianity too has regarded as authentic models of prayer, are full of petitions. And we should not forget that Jesus's Our Father is a prayer of petition and not a selfless glorification of God, and that as well as the heavenly gifts asked for daily bread is mentioned (even in primitive Christianity there was a temptation to interpret it as the bread of eternal life).

When we ask whether and why even man today can genuinely and unaffectedly utter a prayer of petition, and that both in and for his earthly needs, then in my opinion we should, at least at the beginning of theological reflexion on such petitionary prayer, leave aside over-profound and over-subtle theories. These have, incidentally, been dealt with already by traditional theology, as it too, and not only so-called modern man, was familiar with the questions posed by the prayer of petition in particular (apart, that is, from the questions posed by prayer in general). It is reasonable to ask how petitionary prayer is reconcilable with God's omniscience, which does not need us to inform it of our needs, with God's providence and its eternal immutable designs, and with the immutability of God and his will which we are powerless to change.

Illuminating solutions to these and similar problems have been offered. People have asked whether the 'effectiveness' of a prayer of petition for temporal gifts is to be proved empirically, whether, for example, the weather in south Tyrol, with its pious Christian farmers and field processions and blessings of the weather would be different if Tibetan peasants, who do not practise this kind of prayer, were resettled there. If one were a somewhat rationalistic and sceptical Christian, one could also ask what, without being presumptuous, one is to think of the many testimonies of astonishing answers to prayer, from those of places of pilgrimage and the experience of particular pious people and groups to Christian Science. But, as I have said, I shall not properly speak of all this in questioning and defending the prayer of petition.

Only two things must be said to give an understanding of petitionary prayer, and together they seem to me to make the possibility and meaning of petitionary prayer sufficiently intelligible. Firstly, prayer of petition is prayer and meaningful before God only if the desire for a determined and even worldly individual good asked for is also at the same time man's absolute surrender to the sovereign decrees of God's will. One cannot come to God in prayer without giving him oneself, one's whole existence, in trustful submission and love, and in acceptance of the incomprehensible God who is beyond our understanding not only in his essence but also in his free relationship to us and must be accepted as such.

A petitionary prayer which is not thoroughly imbued with Jesus' words before his death: Let your will be done, not mine, is not a petitionary prayer, not a prayer at all, but at most the projection of a vital need into the void, or the attempt to influence God as it were by magic, which is senseless. Only when and in so far as a person gives himself up unconditionally to God and his incomprehensibility, which of course he can do only in faith, hope and especially love, are all goods of a temporal nature for which he petitions properly (= totally) relativized; man acknowledges that the opposite of what is concretely asked for can be salvific too: if, that is, it is granted by God's incomprehensible freedom and accepted by man as God's will.

Man's desire for a determined temporal good is not just brushed aside as of no account, but it is absorbed into that freedom man attains when, because he has surrendered to God, he is dominated by no individual force in his existence. Everything—life and death, health and sickness, power and powerlessness, the past, the present and the future—ceases to be physically or ideologically absolute for man, unconditionally willed or rejected, when he steps before God and lovingly surrenders to him. Praying with genuine prayer, man retains his freedom, unique, ultimate and entire, and also his freedom with regard to what he himself wills with the particular will to existence which governs him. Only in this way is the petition which one tries to direct to God really prayer certain to reach God.

My second statement must be added here. The person who steps into God's presence in this way and yields and entrusts himself unconditionally to his mystery is a concrete person, not an abstract ideal, not a merely religious person who longs for God only. He is a person of daily, profane and banal needs and anxieties. He must place himself before God in prayer just as he is, just as he may permissibly know himself to be: willed by God, in the pressures and needs of his life, which cannot be adequately illumined or simply sublimated into the religious.

This person does not need to have undergone a transformation so that he is in pure harmony with God's decrees—which he does not know and indeed cannot know exactly—before he comes into God's presence. He may, in the act of surrender called prayer, place himself before God just as he is, the one who must give himself to God precisely in his concreteness, the one therefore the pressures and needs of whose life concern some particular thing which seems necessary to him as opposed to something else, and this the more so in that he cannot know whether, with his desire for this particular thing, he is not really willed by God in such a way that this divine willing is willed to be fulfilled in man's concreteness and not merely as a willing sublimated into single-minded surrender. When, however, a person places himself before God as one who as a threatened creature totally submits to God and at the same time wills a particular thing unquestioningly and legitimately, when he is one delivering himself up in his concreteness to God, then he is uttering a prayer of petition. And he does not then need to know exactly *how* the precise relationship of this prayer of petition to God's omniscient and almighty and immutable decree is to be conceived.

It is understandable from this that the prayer of petition is not properly to be thought of as a secondary form of prayer. If it is prayer, it is the loving praise of God (even though not perhaps as explicitly as other forms of prayer specifically couched in doxological terms); if and because it is *petitionary* prayer, it places needy man at his most concrete before God; it is the form of prayer at which man is mindful not only of who *God* is, but also of who *he himself* is. When petitionary prayer is understood in this way, the question of *how* it is granted (if it is granted) is of secondary importance, because a person at prayer should not think he is heard only when his prayer as concrete request is granted in precisely the same way as that in which he had proposed it. Whether one says, referring to the granting of a prayer in the usual sense, that the granting—seen as the granting of *this* prayer—has already been included in the eternal plans of God's providence, or whether one says that it consists in the *salvific* acceptance of the concrete object of prayer, which (at least in the cases where one cannot speak of miracles) in its innerworldly quality as an earthly reality is part of the world's course, which would have proceeded in exactly the same way even without the prayer, these and similar ideas do not seem to me to be so important.

3. THE EXPERIENCE OF GRACE IN DAILY LIFE AND THE EXPLICITNESS OF PRAYER

Let us now return to prayer in general. We can still pray today. This prayer should not be conceived as a (basically supervenient and unconnected) activity in which we indulge 'as well as' in many other activities. It must be understood as the expression and execution of our existence in its entirety, even though explicit prayer might take up only a small part of our time. There is also common prayer, the Church's liturgy. It should not be thought of as second-rank; even the most private prayer must and can be prayed from within that one and common salvation situation which consists in God's approach to the one humanity and the one history of men in his Holy Spirit, and in that one history concerns the individual with the uniqueness of his personal history of freedom and responsibility.

Common liturgical prayer, however, is prayer and not mere ritualism only when the individual really prays in the community, when he really places himself before God as this individual. Prayer, consequently, is not in the least a privatizing, although always and everywhere a private, matter, a realization of the whole of existence—but precisely because of that something which man acquires gradually, something which must be practised and not left to whim and transient emotion. Man cannot force open the ultimate depths of his essence at will, he is frequently exiled to the desolate surface of his own dailiness. Yet prayer is still also a matter of his freedom, responsibility and patient practice.

If, therefore, we have still to say something about prayer and the way in which it can and should be done, it cannot be a question of repeating all the sound and useful and not seldom primitive prescriptions furnished by teachers of the spiritual life, beyond the frontiers of Christianity and the Church, in all major religions. Such prescriptions are basically rules for recollection, for man's concentration on essentials, on that area of his existence for the most part shrouded by what is everyday.

They are intended as helps to effect something approaching an experience of grace—which the experience of the offer of prayer is, and this we should accept in freedom and let it permeate us, not only in the solitude of our 'chamber', separated from men and the world's traffic, but at the centre of life's dailiness, in the ebb and flow of life with its demands, joys and sufferings, its successes and failures. Such an experience at the heart of a totally realized existence proves to the individual the meaningfulness, and indeed the necessity, of prayer. Here man is addressed, called out of himself and moved to prayer by an experience which is more than himself.

In every human life not confined to the visible and tangible or totally absorbed in the needs of the moment, but lived in the Spirit, there are moments and events in which man's whole existence comes into play, in which man is brought up against his life in its entirety, in which the meaning and fulfilment or failure of that life is weighed in the balance: perhaps when a man commits himself to selfless love, or reaches out in yearning and hope for the fulfilment of his life, or is threatened in the depths of his existence. At those moments, attitudes are formed and decisions taken not wholly or rationally explicable in purely innerworldly terms and without an ultimate grounding in the solely here and now; the presence and efficacy of the Spirit is sought—and perhaps also discovered—in a more reflexive way. I shall say something more on this (with due caution and restraint).

Have we ever been silent although we wished to defend ourselves, although we were treated with less than justice? Did we ever forgive although we got no thanks for it and our silent pardon was taken for granted? Did we once obey not because we had to or would otherwise have suffered unpleasant consequences, but merely because of that mysterious, speechless, incomprehensible force we call God and his will? Have we ever made a sacrifice without thanks, acknowledgment or even sentiments of inner peace? Have we ever been thoroughly lonely? Have we had to take a decision purely on the verdict of our conscience, when we cannot tell anybody or explain to anybody, when we are quite alone and know we are making a decision no one can make for us and for which we shall be responsible to eternity? Have we ever tried to love God when no wave of heartfelt enthusiasm sustains us, when we cannot exchange ourselves and life's pressures with God, when we think we are dying of such love, when it feels like death and absolute negation, when we seem to be summoned into the void and the wholly unheard-of, when everything is apparently becoming incomprehensible and seemingly meaningless? Have we perhaps done our duty when we felt we could do it only with the consuming feeling that we were denying ourselves and blotting ourselves out, when we felt we could do it only by perpetrating a horrible stupidity for which no one would thank us? Were we once good to a person from whom no echo of gratitude and understanding returned, and we were not even rewarded with the conviction of having acted 'selflessly', responsibly? And so on.

We can all perhaps see ourselves in such life experiences, or think of our own similar ones. If we can, then we have had the spiritual experience referred to here: the experience of eternity, the experience that spirit is more than a piece of this temporal world, the experience that the meaning of man is not exhausted in the meaning and happiness of this world, the experience of risk and venturesome trust which has no provable justification deducible from mere worldly success, in short and finally: the experience of God, the experience of the descent of the Holy Spirit which became a reality in Christ through his incarnation and his sacrifice on the cross.

If we experience grace-filled spirit in this way and so penetrate that much further into our reflecting consciousness (which of course refers this reflecting objectification and explicitation of the genuine and primitive experience of grace back on to itself), we are at prayer, and our freedom is offered a genuine and explicit prayer. This experience of the Spirit and grace must somehow be expressed by the person who prays if his speech is to be really prayer.

It can, evidently, be that our praying does not arise very lucidly and reflexively in an explicit and 'normal' way from the 'praying' in which God himself is 'leading us in prayer' from the innermost centre of our existence. At such times we might think we are projecting into the void a speech that because it is of our own fabrication rings hollow and substanceless. Even such prayer of honest, daily effort, however, appeals, in the person who has had such an experience of the Spirit of grace (and actually there is no one to whom this has not happened), to this prayer in the depths in which *God* prays our own existence in us, that is, in which God silently draws our existence more and more deeply into his own mystery. Because such spiritual experience still occurs *today*—although perhaps on the sidelines—praying is still possible today.

3 Is prayer dialogue with God?

Every reader of devotional Christian literature and every listener to sermons on prayer is familiar with the statement that prayer is 'a dialogue with God'. Proofs of this commonplace of Christian spirituality and the theology of prayer are not usually adduced expressly. Perhaps it will not come entirely amiss, therefore, to offer some reflexions on the question whether and in what sense prayer can be called a dialogue with God, because the word 'dialogue' would seem to presume that in prayer it is not only man who speaks, but God who speaks too, addresses us and in addressing us answers our word.

The question I am dealing with here, therefore, is not the wider, general question of whether prayer is possible at all and if so what makes it possible, the question in other words of the personal address which man offers to God (not by any means an easy problem today), but the question of whether and in what sense we can say that prayer includes an address of God to man, so that we can properly call prayer a dialogue between God and man.

It is undoubtedly true that man today has great difficulty in understanding and acknowledging that in prayer he experiences something like a personal address on God's part. If we can discount (justifiably in such a short essay as this) the wider question of a personal experience of God as existent and the relationship between God on the one hand, man and the world on the other, in other words, the wider questions which appear more than sufficiently problematic to man today, the difficulty of experiencing prayer as dialogue lies in the fact that what is usually or frequently interpreted in unsophisticated piety as God's address to us at prayer is primarily experienced as one's own psychical state or activity (this is an undoubtedly accurate statement; it certainly cannot be dismissed impatiently today).

The question is consequently how this should be understood as a particular manifestation of God, as his address. The man of today has the impression of to some extent talking to himself in prayer, consulting with himself, even though this self-communion of his is *about* God and his self-reflexion possibly *'before'* God. When he experiences sudden, unexpected and intense new insights and impulses, as does happen, the man of today is more than likely to understand them as movements within his own existence, as suggestions thrown up from the deeper psychic layers, as the breaking out of what has hitherto been repressed, as the fortuitous interplay of subconscious constellations, and so forth. He will refer to the fact that the same perhaps extraordinary psychological phenomena also occur where there is no specifically religious context—in artistic intuitions and ideas, which cannot be programmed, or in sudden changes in personality not motivated by explicitly religious factors, and so on.

We need not inquire here whether he is in fact justified in doing this; the fact remains that man today is under the impression he is being asked to accept a miracle or an outdated mythology when, because of its suddenness, urgency and significance, he is asked to take a powerful, unexpected, psychical happening as the result of a momentary spatio-temporal intervention of God in the normal processes of his consciousness.

It strikes him, at least in general, as no less improbable and incredible in the psychic field than in the external field, where he does not reckon with miracles (in the sense of fresh interventions of God in the world 'from without'). Even when he acknowledges God's existence, he explains the course of his inner world by innerworldly causes, which themselves remain innerworldly even when they produce less common phenomena in the field of his consciousness.

There are, of course, still many people in the Church today, especially in the many 'pentecostal' groups, who interpret particular psychic events—speaking with tongues, baptism of the Spirit, radical conversion, and so on—unashamedly as charismatic interventions of the Holy Spirit 'from without', although this to some extent ignores the fact that all such happenings are primarily *theirs* and (at least until such time as cogent proof of the contrary is offered, and so far it has not been, even by parapsychological phenomena) must be explained as effects of their own internal and external condition. Add to this that to outsiders all such enthusiastic phenomena have their parallels in non-Christian religions which clearly display the peculiarities, horizon of consciousness, speech and limitations of all these psychical causes, and one is hard put to it to discover or know where to look for what necessarily derives from a special, miraculous intervention of God. Because of these and similar considerations, man today finds it very difficult to discover anything in his prayerful consciousness which he could interpret as an address by God distinct from his own mental processes. Prayer seems to him to be a monologue or at best a talking to himself, but not a dialogue with God, an event which one could seriously and without too many reservations call a conversation or an exchange.

In such a difficult situation, one might be tempted to interpret prayer as dialogue with God by saying that it is a discussion (in readings, applications, and so on) with the word of God in revelation and holy scripture. God speaks to us in Scripture; in meditating on Scripture, prayer responds to this word; and there thus arises an exchange, a dialogue with God in prayer. Certainly this view makes some sense to the Christian, who sees Scripture as God's word, but it too has its difficulties. It really succeeds only in putting the problem a stage further back, because revelation accepted by man's spirit (if it is not, of course, it is not revelation) and revelation objectified in Scripture raise basically the same question: how can the content of a human consciousness, which in consciousness has become a part of man's subjectivity and suffers from all its limitations, and is ultimately to be interpreted as the effect of this human causality, be heard and understood as the word of God? Even discounting this serious problem (which we cannot pursue further here), there is still another difficulty in this view.

In prayer, a devout Christian believes he is the recipient of an actual address from God calling him in his individuality and individual life's decision. If, however, this Christian has to regard the application of the word of Scripture, which in itself is universal, to himself and the actual situation of his life as his own work undertaken at his own expense and peril, as the application therefore of merely universal norms to a concrete situation of individual decision whose 'more' over and above the universal is still precisely that on which it depends, no such dialogue would take place, as however is maintained by one who conceives of prayer as a dialogue. All that remains is a merely human application of a divine word of universal significance to an individual and the concrete, ever-unique questions of his life.

A man at prayer is still only talking to himself, even though

he enjoys the assistance of a universal divine word. The passage
from universal revelation to the concrete imperative is solely
man's work, and even though he thought of it as (in part) the
work of divine grace, it is not clear how he could interpret this
help from grace in the application of the word of Scripture to
himself and the questions of his life as a divine address because of
which the concrete imperative (which calls to the man who prays)
could be understood as the call of God.

It is true that assistance from such grace in actual decision is
understood in theology as 'illumination' and 'inspiration', but it
is still questionable what precisely this statement means, in that
there is at least one great school of theology which interprets this
illumination and inspiration, in so far as it is the condition of
salvific acts, as merely 'entitative' and beyond consciousness, and
therefore claims that nothing is added to the understanding of an
address by God in prayer.

Even if it were said that such a process of prayer, in which a
salvific decision is taken, as well as being supported by supernatural grace is accompanied by 'medicinal' graces which urge
this event to a concluding, salvific decision, I have not advanced
any further into my question. That is because this medicinal
grace is interpreted as the result of innerworldly causes in itself
and therefore also primarily, and the same difficulty from which
I started in my question about the possibility of being addressed by
God in prayer therefore remains. Even this medicinal grace is part
of innerworldly reality in the web of causes and effects, can therefore, like everything else in the world, be understood as God's free
creation through which God intends our salvation, but not as
God's address any more than anything else in our history.

I suppose that many people make my question easy for themselves by first taking as given the knowledge of the personalness
of God, and then promptly concluding that we can address him.
Having got so far in the argument, one is under the impression of
already standing in a relationship of direct, actualizable dialogue.
However, even when one presumes that God is to be thought of as
'personal' in and for himself, the other two steps to actual dialogue with God are not justified: that the personal God can be
addressed by us remains obscure; and that he answers such an
address and is not silent has particularly to be clarified. Even
when one says, with regard to the second step, that God has
abandoned his silence, spoken to us in his verbal revelation and
communicated with us, the same question recurs: why the exchange in prayer is more than a conversation with oneself about
the universal revelation of God in his history of revelation, more

than mere application of this revelation to one's own situation at one's own expense and peril.

I must try to proceed in another direction. The presupposition, up to now regarded as self-evident, underlying our reflexions on prayer as dialogue with God is that God says 'something' to us *in* prayer. The presupposition of my problem was that a particular individual, categorial content of consciousness—one of many—in a special and distinctive way effected directly by God and grasped in this special causality, constituted something like a dialogue with God. This presumption raised the difficulty I have already mentioned. How would it be, however, if we said and were permitted to say that in prayer we experience ourselves as the ones spoken by God, as the ones arising from and decreed by God's sovereign freedom in the concreteness of our existence? If we said that what God primarily says to us is ourselves in our decreed freedom, in our decree-defying future, in the facticity (that can never be totally analyzed and never functionally rationalized) of our past and present?

If we understand my question in this way, it is of course understood that the relationship of 'partnership' and 'dialogue' between God and us is unique and incomparable and cannot simply be thought of univocally on the model of an interhuman relationship of partnership and dialogue. Consequently the concept of 'dialogue' for our question must have a unique and incomparable quality if it is to indicate the distinctiveness of prayer. If we can answer the newly-posed question in the affirmative, we are ourselves (in our transcendentality, which is experienced as such at its origin, as we might say) the utterance and address of God which listens to itself. That, however must not be understood merely as a general statement, but as a statement about present existence in its wholly determined, unique and historical actuality, given up to itself and *therefore* experiencing itself as spoken to itself by God.

God's most original word to us in our free uniqueness is not a word arising momentarily and categorially in addition to or separate from other objects of experience within a wider area of our consciousness, but is we ourselves as integral, total entities and in our reference to the incomprehensible mystery we call God, the word of God which we ourselves are and which as such is spoken to us. As soon as these phrases, which are at first sight of merely existential-ontological significance, are taken in conjunction with the presupposition that this transcendentality is already and everywhere (because of God's universal salvific will) raised and radicalized by virtue of God's immediacy by what we call supernatural grace as God's self-communication, then such phrases are seen to be directly theological.

When a person, in the Spirit and by grace, experiences himself as the one spoken by God to himself and understands this as his true essence to the concreteness of which the gratuitous grace of God's self-communication also belongs, and when he admits this existence and freely accepts it in prayer as the word of God in which God promises himself to man with his Word, his prayer is already (in one sense, to be elaborated later) dialogic, an exchange with God. The person then hears himself as God's address, heavy with God's self-promise, in the grace-filled self-communication of God by faith, hope and love. He does not hear 'something' in addition to himself as one already presupposed in his dead facticity, but hears himself as the self-promised word in which God sets up a listener and to which he speaks himself as an answer.

Obviously it cannot be my business here to ground the statements just formulated in a theological and philosophical anthropology. If it could be, care would have to be taken that the statements were not merely uttered and substantiated as affirmations reaching man and given to him only when he thinks and talks about them in subsequent statements. They should rather be understood and proved as transcendental: that is, here, simply as statements whose content is always and everywhere realized and known in and together with man's spiritual and free self-realization as the unthematic conditions of the possibility of all human existence, so that then this transcendentally dialogical existence can be taken up into prayer, partially thematized and accepted in reflexive freedom, and prayer itself understood as a dialogue. As I have said, however, these statements cannot here be either explained more precisely or substantiated more accurately.

However, so far I have named only one aspect—the 'transcendental'—of prayer from which prayer as dialogue becomes intelligible in a particular sense. I must add to this a second, from which the usual understanding of prayer as an exchange is given some justification as well as purified of mythological and miraculous misunderstanding. If man unconditionally and unfeignedly accepts his absolute openness to God (which is God's most original word to man), given by God and his freedom, if it is not hidden, distorted and misused by a free predecision of man to wholly determined categorial contents of his consciousness, then (the reader will, I hope, permit this perhaps apparently arbitrary jump in thought) arises what Ignatius of Loyola calls in his *Exercises* 'indifference' and (if this indifference is really realized and sustained in radical freedom) 'consolation without preceding cause'.

If a particular individual object of choice now becomes part of such an ultimate dialogical freedom, without disguising, confusing or restricting, even in the course of further spiritual experience and questioning, this pure openness to God, it is experienced as the means by which this indifferent openness to God in unconditional surrender to him, and therefore (to put it the other way round) in unconditional acceptance of God's word which we ourselves are, is accepted and maintained, and this categorial object of choice (however conditioned and innerworldly in itself) can and may be conceived as a moment of this dialogical relationship between God and man because and in so far as this object is inserted into the conversational dialogue as a whole without jeopardizing or abrogating the latter's unlimited and unconditioned openness. From a purely innerworldly and categorial, objective point of view, such a categorial object of choice on which a man decides in prayer can still be problematic and perhaps later, compared with man's innerworldly needs and structures, be seen to be inadequate, provisional, ephemeral, even harmful; but here and now it is the best mediation of this indifferent, transcendental openness in which man experiences himself as God's word in promise, and therefore is God's salvific will.

In such a logic of existential knowledge and freedom, prayer becomes dialogical even in its categorial character as a succession of individual contents. That which enters our consciousness with rich sentimental feeling or with a suddenness and unexpectedness that leaves us breathless, is not so alone in being considered the effect of the Spirit and so as God's address that it has to be enthusiastically defended against a hardheaded and sceptical psychology. Rather, where the particular, consciously appropriated reality on which one decides can serve as a positive mediation of a permanent and unconditional openness to God (we could also say: of an unconditioned critical freedom), such a particular object may be understood as spoken to us by God in and with that fundamental address of God to ourselves which we ourselves are and which we perceive and accept in prayer.

It is not maintained here that the two aspects of prayer I have just tried briefly to indicate adequately constitute the dialogical character of prayer. I should be happy if the reader agreed I had at least clarified it a little further. And of course I cannot now clarify the consequences of such an understanding of prayer as exchange. It is possible that it now seems even harder than one usually thinks to understand prayer seriously and soberly as a conversation with God, and especially to experience it in practice as a conversation now that it has been 'demythologized'. If this is so, I am not saying that the normal believer should have reflexively before his mind in unreflected everyday life all the considerations I have put forward. After following such reflexions and feeling disillusioned, he may experience prayer as a dialogue with God—because that is what it is—in a new sort of naïvety.

Note: For further exploration of several topics raised here, see *Sacramentum Mundi* (six vols., London & New York (1968–70) and *Encyclopedia of Theology: a concise Sacramentum Mundi* (London & New York, 1975), especially the articles on Prayer, Experience and Meditation; as well as my *Theological Investigations (passim)*.

4 The *Exercises* today

1. Even today the *Spiritual Exercises* (of St Ignatius of Loyola) must still be (although this does not exhaust their specific essence) *a time of solitude and prayer* because a time of personal encounter with God. They are intended to foster *decision and choice*. The material content of choice can ripen in an 'encounter with the world' and extend to political decisions, but this alters nothing in the decision's formal (generic) character as 'lonely' decision, as loneliness and prayer.

This is philosophically and Christianly justified because an individual person is never just a mere function of a community, not even of the Church. That does not prejudge the question of how far a discreetly appointed meeting with others (apart from the master of the *Exercises*) can, or even must (today), be used as a particular means during this solitary period. The *Exercises* demand only that their user take and accept himself in his ultimate permanent solitude before God, and they must therefore expose flight into the masses (even ecclesial), not encourage it.

2. The *Exercises* are exercises in choice and decision *before God, to God, in* Christ and his grace, otherwise they are not exercises. They therefore presuppose and existentially *put into practice* the fundamental substance of Christianity: that the living, incomprehensible God exists, that we have a personal relationship with him in freedom and by grace, a relationship which despite all mediation (through and in Christ, and from Christ through the whole width of worldly existence) is immediate (*on both sides*), that this relationship to God in prayer and decision can and must become thematic and is not just the unthematic, hidden ground of a relationship to the world. The *Exercises* presuppose that there is an existential decision through an individual call of God to the actual person. To be credible today, therefore, the logic of the

existential decision ('discernment of spirits') and the concept of a revelation of God by means of a personal, individual address (and incidentally the concept of revelation in general) must be 'de-mythologized', and the exercitand (or person practising the *Exercises*) brought to experience such a divine address in a way that is both sober and genuinely acceptable today. It must there-fore be made clear to the exercitand that the *Exercises* are not the abstract indoctrination of a theoretical doctrinal system with all its 'practical' consequences (to which point of view Jesuit intellectualism and anti-Ignatian juridicism have inclined in centuries past), but an initiation into man's religious experience and sanctification from within.

From this it follows that a commentary on the *Exercises* must include not only a developed theology of the dogmatic, objective statements of the *Exercises*, but offer a (formal) theology of the existential experience of grace and of the 'psychological' (what a misleading word that can be) instructions to facilitate a more lucid and more explicitly accepted experience. There need be no fear of infringing the nature of this experience as grace, provided only that it is understood that this grace is *always* offered, that it can take on the *most disparate* forms of experience, that a non-decision (a 'silence of God') can also be a grace-given experience, and so on. It follows from this that the *Exercises* are *essentially* exercises for *individuals*. Group exercises can to some extent avail themselves of the name only if they are so constructed that they provide a serious context for the growth of an individual religious history.

3. The perception and acceptance of a divine call in decision (in 'choice') always has—corresponding to the nature of man and Christianity—two unified, mutually conditioned aspects: one 'transcendental' and one 'categorial', the aspect of radical decision for God (as its aim) *and* the mediating realization of this decision in a concrete demand and mission of historical life: *metanoia*, or conversion to God, in faith, hope and love on the one hand *and* the concreteness of this *metanoia* in a particular real situation as demand for a particular act (the shaping of life, the choice of vocation, love of one's neighbour, the endurance of life's distasteful dailiness with its pressures, and so on) on the other. These aspects cannot be separated; but their reciprocal relation-ship is not static and cannot be theoretically tabulated, but has a history of an individual and epochal nature and must therefore be again and again determined in historical decision (of the Church in a given period, of the individual in his life).

4. Several points follow logically from this.

(*a*) The fundamental relationship of immediacy to God (the transcendental aspect of every decision and the choice realized and deepened in this or that particular choice, in other words the ever new metanoia as such) cannot *today* be simply presumed as given either theoretically (as the self-evident givenness of an institutionally powerful Christianity with its indisputable public opinion) or existentially (as the uncontested inner faith of the individual), as if the *Exercises* had to deal solely with the concrete choice under its categorial aspect ('what does God's will, which is self-evident, hold for me here and now?'). In this respect, the situation of the *Exercises* is essentially different from that of Ignatius' time, even in so-called believing and 'practising' Catholics who very often brush aside and do not really master the fact that their belief is contested.

The *Exercises* today must consequently take this situation much more lucidly and deliberately into consideration, under every aspect: in the choice and composition of their thematic material with the help of which the choice is to be made, in their consideration of the religious situation of the exercitand today, which blocks the religious experience and threatens him precisely when he does not thematically (consciously) accept it or brushes it to one side (as, for example, many of an older generation of religious orders did), and in their language. This does not mean that the *Exercises* should be turned into a course in theoretical problematic on the essence of Christianity and its credibility today.

The *Exercises* master, however, must bear all this in mind in his initiation into the basic religious experience and its believing, radical acceptance in the course of the exercitand's confrontation with his real concrete question of life (usually to be discovered for the first time) which calls him to a decision. In consequence, especially the question of the structure and articulation of the thematic of the considerations proposed in the *Exercises* must be posed in a radically new way. The question can perhaps be solved by a bold differentiation and contradistinction in the order of the *Exercises* as proposed by Ignatius. It could also be, however, that (at least for certain exercitands) radical changes in the thematic itself are necessary and justified. Today a longer and more explicit *introduction* to the point at which Ignatius allows the exercitand to begin the *Exercises* is probably nearly always necessary.

(*b*) Despite (because of) what was said under (*a*), the *Exercises* are and remain choice and decision in a concrete life situation and not a mere theoretical initiation into the essence of Christianity.

This is not only because they have been so understood historically, but particularly because the basic, total *metanoia* (fundamental option), which is not just a theoretical—and not concretely possible only as theoretical—cultivation of Christianity, is possible only in the concrete life situation and that situation's origin in decision. (What has today become) the *Exercises'* obligation mentioned under (a) above does not, therefore, contradict the old object of the *Exercises*. On the contrary, man will come to know what is really meant by God, sin, grace, forgiveness, Christ, discipleship of Christ, cross, only in a question of actual existence posed concretely, faced squarely and not brushed aside, and accepted in free responsibility.

Therefore, if an initiation into existentially accepted Christianity in faith, hope and love for God is not to remain abstract indoctrination (whatever its depth of theological insight), if it is to try and extract this concrete situation as one of decision from the shrouded, marginal position it at present occupies in the exercitand's consciousness, it must be able to awaken both Christianity as a whole *and* a personal decision grounded on it.

Again the question arises of the theology and initiation technique ('psychology') of such a confrontation of the exercitand with his life's question which demands to be answered here and now and which very often lies somewhere other than he himself at first suspects. For Ignatius (as the giver of the *Exercises*, not so much for himself, in his own decision and choice, as his 'memoirs' show) the genuine objects of choice were usually given openly (as the various vocations pregiven and preformed by the Church and society). Today they have first to be found, and given the complexity of man today lie much more deeply hidden than previously.

5. Any commentary on the text of the *Exercises* must devote itself equally explicitly to the content of the affirmations and to the methodological instructions. The apparently merely methodological-psychological instructions of the text raise more than psychological problems: they often imply a whole theology; commenting them therefore is *also* a properly theological undertaking. The commentary should not be an edifying paraphrase of the text, as we have been used to in our *Exercises*.

There must be some rigorous questioning: what does this mean? does that exist? can a man of today really understand the other? where will he find by his own devices an intellectual access to all that is expressed here in an almost archaic and apparently mythological way? what are the presuppositions underlying the text, which we today can no longer presume to be self-evident, but have to set out explicitly to recapture? and so on. All this applies equally to the theological content of the text's affirmations and its methodological instructions and rules.

5 Penance and confession

A dogmatic theologian should really say more on the theme of penance and confession than is possible here. That should be borne in mind if the choice of points selected for discussion in what follows seems somewhat arbitrary. The basic lines of Catholic doctrine on the sacrament of confession are taken as known and binding.

1. According to the Gospel and the teaching of the Church, penance in the sense not so much of an isolated, intermittently posited activity as of a basic attitude determining the whole of Christian existence, in the sense therefore of a basic *metanoia* (conversion to God through faith and contrition) continually renewed, is a grace from God and a charge on man as an individual and on the Church as a whole. It has to be asked whether this permanent *metanoia* in the individual, which means basically *both* change of mind *and* change of external behaviour together with the institutions, has not been narrowed down to too individualistic an assurance of salvation, and whether this permanent *metanoia* in the Church as a whole has been misinterpreted as an *aggiornamento* which is certainly necessary but which never matches the radicality of ecclesial *metanoia* as it should be experienced.

2. This situation in the life of the individual Christian and of the Church today is made worse by the fact that the understanding of the Christian significance of sin and forgiveness of sin must be re-acquired and re-expressed so that modern man's temptation to unfetter his relationship to God as a sinner by appealing to his genetic, psychological and social conditioning and finitude can be met in the right place and in the right way. This is because these attempts at unshackling the relationship are in themselves justified, but do not erase the more radical basic experience of being referred to God's grace as a sinner.

The Church, however, must recognize that it is faced here with a new challenge to which so far in its preaching, catechesis and initiation into basic religious experience it has not sufficiently adverted.

3. The dogmatic theologian must clearly emphasize (as also when dealing with public worship) that he would be stunting theology and the Christian understanding of existence to an unacceptable degree if he maintained that, to the extent that the process of penance (as *metanoia*) in the life of the Christian impinges on the ecclesial sphere or even in general, it is limited to the reception of the sacrament of penance in the sense of individual confession. The following can be just as much salvific events of metanoia, provided that they are recognized (more or less thematically) as God's work and are experienced (again, more or less thematically) as God-given, as the grace of forgiveness and the bestowal of life: genuine acts of self-criticism, of 'revision of life', of the avowal of guilt, of the plea for pardon (where it has not degenerated into a cheap process of self-exoneration or a social stunt), of the rejection of social conventionalisms and institutionalisms with which one has up to now identified oneself to one's own advantage; the admission of a social self-manifesting 'movement' which one has up to then tried to obstruct out of indolence or egoism; a readiness to confront the harsh truths in one's own existence—which the keener gaze of psychology and depth psychology today reveal—about one's own poverty in relationships, one's egoism, one's false introversion, pseudo-forms of the religious, false taboos of the sexual and so on; and many other partial manifestations of conversion and breakthrough in human maturity and of the assumption of one's own interhuman and social responsibility. To this extent the (individual and collective) elimination of cliché-ridden and stagnant forms of what is really meant by penance is to be regarded as a legitimate process which is itself a part of *metanoia*.

4. Even the sacrament of penance itself can escape a purely legalistic or even ultimately magical misinterpretation only if it is understood, administered and received as a particular concretization of this metanoia in the context of the Church. The clearer and more convincing this concretization of *all* the dimensions of penance, and the less attempt made simply to dispose of a single sinful occurrence in the past, the more prospect there is for the sacrament to be appreciated and made use of today.

5. Discerning and realizing at their roots the ecclesiological aspects of sin and forgiveness of sin reflects not only the necessary understanding of man's social dimension today but the teaching

of the second Vatican council. It must not be undertaken as merely theoretical ideology on the occasion of the reception of the sacrament, but must be clear in the actual structure of the sacrament in general. There must be an inner unity, not just competition, between penitential services and particular receptions of the sacrament.

6. The interpretation, theologically unanimous since Thomas Aquinas, of the yearly duty of confession universally laid down by the fourteenth Lateran council nearly 750 years ago has also been prominent in catechism classes and popular religious instruction. It states that the Easter duty is properly a commandment of the Church's human law only when there are sins not yet submitted sacramentally to God's forgiveness which, both objectively *and subjectively*, are such as, in biblical language (Gal. 5:21; 1 Cor. 6:9; etc.), to exclude from the kingdom of God. Of course the duty to submit such grave sins to the sacramental consolation of the Church's pardon, because of the nature of sin, of the Church and of the sacrament of penance, refers to 'grave sins' thus understood, even independently of the humanly issued commandment of the Church, in so far as God's forgiveness of these sins must be salvation-historically, salvifically, sacramentally and ecclesially manifested at some time or other in the life of the sinner through the act of the Church. The determined period of time in which this fundamental duty is to be fulfilled is of human law in the Church; in principle it could be abrogated and certainly must, like every other human law, be so construed and applied in the Church that it serves man's salvation and not his ruin.

7. Contrary to a trend in moral theology over the centuries (from perhaps as early as the Irish, Anglo-Saxon and Merovingian books of penance), there is no reason, in either dogma or religious and popular education, either with regard to the extent of the objective grave matter or with regard to the presumption of the extent of the sins committed subjectively as grave, to follow the rigorism which at least since the post-Tridentine period has predominated in moral theology and the practice of the sacrament of penance until today. Such rigorism, both in determining the extent of the *materia gravis* and in presuming that an infringement of the law in a *materia objective gravis* more or less always involves a subjectively grave guilt in the normal Christian, cannot be theologically substantiated. The presumption that there are sins which are subjectively very grave and therefore liable to the strict duty of confession in Christians who are living a life of basic church-Christian practice is also a position that is open to severe doubt. Consequently the frequency of grave sins which

must necessarily be submitted to the forgiveness of sacramental confession has to be judged within a church of people who seriously desire to live a Christian life.

Now, as the experience of the Church in patristic and early medieval times shows, if the only sins submitted in confession are grave ones, the confession of such sins, at least in the form of the sacrament customary today, becomes psychologically very difficult if not in practice impossible, except perhaps on one's death-bed. Hence (leaving out of account here other psychological and similar reasons) an unnuanced and indiscreet propaganda for the opinion that only sins which absolutely need sacramental confession should in fact be included in particular confession is to be rejected. The reception of the sacrament of penance in particular confession retains its justification and its usefulness today (given the necessary reservations to be clarified below) even when sins that absolutely speaking do not need to be confessed are in fact confessed.

Precisely when one feels, for reasons which cannot be enlarged on here, that a too clear-cut distinction between grave and venial sins, as is customary in the average moral theology and church practice, is too facile and legalistic (even though such a distinction is sometimes correct and indispensable), then one has no proper grounds (unless one is going to deny the sacrament of penance itself) for canvassing the view that only grave sins, even where subjectively certain, should be submitted in particular confession. Nevertheless, *avoiding* such propaganda does not depend on acting as if every Christian were under a strict duty in church law to go to confession at least once a year even though he is aware of no serious sins.

8. It seems to me to be still certain today that according to the teaching of the Council of Trent the duty of receiving the sacrament of penance for objectively and subjectively really serious sins refers to particular confession, which in this case cannot be replaced by a penitential service of a general nature, even when that service is intended to be sacramental and so structured, and even though such a sacramental absolution with no more than a general confession may eventually, with or without alteration in the Church's positive command, be legitimately substituted for an actual particular confession.

If the real extent of objectively and subjectively grave sins is not arbitrarily enlarged with a thoughtless rigorism, in a form of the sacrament of penance which respects human and liturgical norms, the Tridentine specification of particular confession (and with it the commandment of the Church as laid down in Lateran

IV) is still humanly, religiously, liturgically and pastorally justi-
fiable today. Only, however, on these premises. If these premises
are not fulfilled, then of course one can foresee a drop in the use
of particular confession which would exceed the limits of the
dogmatically binding and what is Christianly, humanly and
pastorally correct. That is not to deny that there is also a drop in
the frequency of particular confession due to the conditions of the
period in which we live and based on a certain change in the
relationship of the Christian to the sacraments in general, on the
complexity of human life for which advice in the confessional is
less easily given than before, on a change in the relationship
between pastor and Christian, and similar factors into which I
cannot enter here.

9. A general penitential service should not be regarded as a
substitute for particular confession, which makes forgiveness more
equitable and technically more manageable. Where it is valued in
the religious feeling of the average Christian *solely* as just such a
substitute, it need only lose the attraction of novelty and it has
both weakened the habit of particular confession and become
itself but seldom practised. Penitential services can still be an independent form of penance in the Church because of the nature of
sin, the social conditionality and effect of sin, and the nature of
the *Ecclesia semper poenitens*. Sometimes, too, it can be a much
greater help to personal *metanoia* for the individual than particular confession, which, because of the number of penitents, the
pressures on today's clergy, and one's psychological, psychothera-
peutic (and not seldom also religiously weak) experience, has less
genuinely religious significance for an initiation into true
metanoia.

If other necessary conditions are observed, and with the above-
mentioned proviso with relation to the duty to confess sins which
are both objectively *and* subjectively grave, a priestly absolution
can have sacramental significance for the individual even in a
general community confession. I do not really believe that this
sacramental quality can be absent if the priest, who pronounces
God's forgiveness as the representative of the Church, sincerely
means what he says. Such a sacramental quality seems to me to be
present even when the priest leading the penitential service and
pronouncing pardon over the community does not expressly
reflect on the sacramentality of what he is doing or even perhaps
thinks he can exclude it. An explicit declaration of the service's
sacramental nature because the service is conducted by the official
Church would be desirable, but it does not seem to me to be a
necessary condition for the penitential service to be sacramental.

10. These services of penance should not, however, or at least not merely, be, almost in the style of a sensitivity group or the Salvation Army or any pentecostal movement, the common cultivation of a conversion and purification event still ultimately experienced as an individual event, but must take up and embrace in a Christian way the secular ethos of an increasingly effective responsibility of the individual within a society as such. In this way they could really become the actual manifestation of the self-realization of the Church as the body called to true and constant *metanoia* and to a self-realization in which, more clearly than Thomas Aquinas could envisage, the Church as the concrete, even though officially structured, community also becomes the sacramental bearer of the manifestation of man's conversion and God's forgiveness, and ecclesial penance really becomes the penance of the Church itself. The question then immediately arises: what sort of community must it be to be the real, genuine bearer of this realization of *metanoia*? This in turn raises a vital question of pastoral theology today: the question of the basic group, of the integrated community, of the community of Christians genuinely fashioned on the reality of life as opposed to mere administrative units of the Church's institution, a question therefore which at best can only very indirectly become the object of a dogmatic inquiry.

6 Lent

The idea of preparing for the annual feast of Easter with forty days of fasting (a number held sacred since scriptural times) instead of a week (as in up to the third century) prevailed in the East towards the end of the fourth century. Rome did not accept the idea of a forty-day fast before Easter until the seventh century. Since then this 'Quadragesima' has remained in both East and West, though with modified significance.

What meaning can we give to the idea today? Has Lent any significance at a time when a modern industrial society takes no notice of it (and hardly can)? It cannot properly be the time for baptism candidates and public penitents any more. And what does 'preparation' for Easter mean: days of silence? preparation of the heart for the renewal of the baptismal vows on Easter night? 'annual Spiritual Exercises for the community'? All these motivations behind Lent are justified and meaningful, and they can certainly be elaborated and developed.

However, could we not apply the sort of 'Copernican revolution' in modern piety, which is justified and based on the unequivocal dogma of the Church, to the significance, the 'theology', of Lent too? To explain what I mean, I must begin further back.

Catholic doctrine has always known that not only are the explicit devotional exercises (prayer, reception of the sacraments, works of penance, and so on) 'meritorious', that is, events of growth in grace, of maturity in Christian-moral personhood, of man's movement to his ultimate end in the beatific vision of God, but that the same may be said of all works which he performs daily 'in a state of grace' if they are freely posited and not sins. For the earlier devotional life of the average Christian, however, this teaching was not really a conviction determining his actual life. Properly religious life, in which man has something to do with

God and God with him, did not begin until he had proceeded
beyond the profane world and secular life to the point at which
he began to pray and grow in grace through receiving the sacraments, at which he turned to God in a reflexive way through
petitionary prayer, almsgiving and (partly meaningful, partly
superstitious) religious customs, 'religious folklore'. A sublimer
spiritual teaching knew something, certainly, of 'good intentions'
which enabled a person to sanctify the deeds and sufferings of his
daily life, but for the average Christian that was no more than a
distant theory, and even in this teaching 'good intentions' seemed
mostly to be little more than an external addition by which a
wholly profane work, which remained wholly profane, could still
become 'meritorious'. There were two worlds: the earthly, profane world in which normal man spent most of his time willy
nilly, and a religious world—appended as a heterogeneous
element, fostered mainly by priests and nuns ('religious people')—
which people 'in the world' could only with difficulty and in small
doses bring to bear on their secular existences.

Today Christianity is slowly learning that it can and must live
and understand everything in profane life as a process of salvation
(or unsalvation) if it is not to incur a false secularism such as
appears to be in vogue today. Everything that is not sin but is
freely and responsibly posited is, for the Christian in a state of
grace, an event of this grace, a piece of salvation history borne up
by the Spirit of God, an acceptance of his eternity. What we
usually call 'the religious life' and anachronistically regard as an
addition (even if a necessary one) to profane life, is in fact the
reflexive, individual and social coming-to-itself *of* the life of grace
which evolves at the heart of 'profane' life and is only the obverse
of profane life (provided, of course, that it is not a sinful No to
God); it is an explicit and reflexive acceptance of the personal
salvation history which unfolds in the daily life of the individual.
When, in prayer, we expressly 'awaken' the 'theological virtues'
of faith, hope and charity to God and our neighbour, we are not
supplementing our profane life with the virtues, but making *this*
faith, *this* hope and *this* charity, which permeate our life if it is
truly Christian, clear to ourselves in an explicitly formulated way.
When we celebrate the Lord's death in the Eucharist, we are
celebrating the passion of Jesus in which we share 'anonymously'
in the passion and death of our own lives. When we perform an
'act of hope' by 'supernatural' grace, it is a 'ratification' of that
'perseverance' and 'not despairing' which animate the daily round
and possess an unconditionedness *in* that daily round which longs
for an infinite satisfaction. And so on.

Is it now clear what is meant by the 'Copernican revolution' in modern piety? It consists in the experience that the real depth of the apparently superficial and 'worldly' dailiness of life is filled and can be filled with God and his grace, and that because of this ultimate meaning of apparently secular life, the expressly religious becomes intelligible and practicable for the men of our time. Conversely, of course, it cannot be denied that if the expressly religious is genuinely practised, it in its turn illuminates this anonymous Christianness of the secular daily round.

The same may be said of Lent. Lent is the religious explicitness of that period of 'fast' and 'passion' which extends over our whole lives. Today's welfare and consumer State has accommodated itself to a permanent lie: the impression is universally given that serene happiness is everywhere the rule, or if that is not strictly true in every case, it soon will be with good will and the irresistible progress of mankind. Evidently no one would wish to quarrel with the ideals of more health, wealth, freedom and so on by which modern man sets such store. The fact is that many things remain: pain, old age, sickness, disappointment in marriage, in the children, in one's job, and at the end of it all death, which no one escapes and which is already a controlling, permeating factor of life. The question can consequently be only *how* one is to cope with this reality of suffering and death.

Cynicism and stoicism do not go very far. In faith, hope and love a Christian understands this aspect of his life as a sharing in the Lord's passion. The acceptance in belief and hope of one's own passion is exercised by what in Christian asceticism is called 'voluntary renunciation'. In Lent, however, that which one must necessarily suffer in life in sober realism and can live in hope as a *Christian* passion becomes publicly known, in ecclesial, liturgical and sacramental explicitness, as a freely-loving participation in the passion of Christ.

7 The theology of dying

An American-Swiss psychiatrist, Elisabeth Kubler-Ross, wrote a book on death and dying which caused something of a sensation a few years ago. The book speaks of the anguish of death, of the ways in which the dying can relate to dying and death, of the dying person's family; it offers a large number of interviews with sick people on their death-beds; it speaks of the psychological behaviour of the sick at death's door. It has no directly religious intentions, although it reports without bias the interviews with several of the dying who expressed Christian religious attitudes to death. I am not going to review the book here, either to praise or to criticize it. I wish simply to offer a theological reflexion on a twofold observation it makes.

The book distinguishes five stages in the reaction of a sick person to the knowledge that he is going to die: refusal to admit it and the attempt to insulate himself from it; anger; discussion; depression; acquiescence. A theological remark may usefully be made here on this fifth and final stage (which is 'normal') in the dying person's reaction to the knowledge of his condition, on the acquiescence, therefore, or agreement with death. Even in this last stage, despite the acquiescence in death reported by Elisabeth Kubler-Ross, the sick person always retains a certain last hope to which he holds even at this fifth stage. My theological reflexion is to consider this fifth stage.

It goes without saying for a Christian theology of dying and death that the eternal destiny of a dying person, which becomes definitive in death, can never be deduced with unequivocal certainty from the circumstances of dying accessible to the observation of bystanders, but remains the secret of human freedom and of God. This is presumed here and must not be forgotten. Correspondingly it is not disputed either that the so-called last stage of dying, that of humble acceptance, can have causes (the physiological helplessness of the dying, for example) which as far as external observation goes have nothing to do with the dying person's free and responsible decision. However (and it is this which concerns us here), the act of acquiescence can, despite its incontestable physiological postulates, still be the act in which there is a free acceptance on the part of the dying person, in which the person really lets go of himself and of everything to which he had hitherto held on as a particular good in an absolute, free decision; this acquiescence can therefore be an act in which the person surrenders himself to the will of the incomprehensible God, in which, even though perhaps very implicitly, he 'repents of his sins' because in this acquiescence he also surrenders those goods to which he had up to that moment culpably adhered in unconditional freedom.

This fifth stage in dying (Kubler-Ross) could therefore also have a supreme religious and theological significance. That does not mean that this acquiescence necessarily and always occurs *as* salvific, that a person's salvation is assured because in dying he experiences just such a phase of acceptance in which his life is of itself aligned on God. Apart from everything else, this is true because a sudden and possibly violent death presumably does not contain any such phase of acceptance. But, conversely, one may well still accept that in a 'normal' five-stage dying there is a situation in which God's merciful providence makes it easy for a man to leave 'the world', to renounce a sinful attachment to it and to surrender confidently to that incomprehensible mystery which in death man meets more clearly than ever before and which we call God. This is all the more probable in that, as I have already said, the acceptance is always accompanied by a last hope. If it is theologically interpreted, this hope does not need to be understood as the last spark of a merely earthly hope which is quite extinguished when death brings the dying to an end.

This hope in every acceptance of dying can also be understood as the resonance of the 'hope against all hope' (Rom. 4 : 18) in which the person reaches out unconditionally to his absolute future, God. Because, as we could perhaps say, man possesses an unconditional hope at the very heart of his existence which he can deny only in the mortal guilt of despair, he also hopes in earthly hope as long as he lives.

Unlike many theologians today (for example, Ladislaus Boros), we need not mystify death on the assumption that there is in every possible case at the precise moment of death a total decision on one's definitive destiny and the ultimate and definitive Yes or No to God. We can, however, assume that a normal dying can at least be a situation in which the temporary is quietly taken from man and the silent infinity of God is offered, in which it becomes relatively easy for the person to turn the last deed of his life to his eternal salvation. We cannot know, only hope, of course, that this fifth stage in the process of dying is a salvation situation also for those people who are only 'anonymous' Christians and die as such, people who do not explicitly share the Christian faith but are men of good will, in whose hearts grace works unseen and who are therefore united with the Easter mystery of Christ's death even if in a way known only to us.

8 Hope and Easter

At the start two things must be said. Firstly, I am—at least I hope
I am—convinced in faith of the truth of the Christian Easter
message. With the Christian churches I confess that *the Lord is
truly risen*: that and nothing else, however much I am aware
that at all times and therefore also today one must meditate on
what it means. I do not intend to speak of it in a way acceptable
to all: that would be to say nothing of value. I think nonetheless
that such a clear confession is still worth thinking about for *all*
men today—because of the subject, naturally, not because of the
writer. And secondly: the following is not an attempt at a prose
poem or Easter hymn. Believers who can leave despair and the
disillusionment of life behind them, who believe and who, freed
by this inner blessing of their lives, confess what they believe, sing
that hymn. My purpose here is not so much to speak of this
hoping Easter faith itself as to offer a modest meditation at its
margin, at its threshold, on its meaning and credibility. Belief
and such reflexions on it are not the same thing.

Many (perhaps most) people *live* an ultimate conviction because
of which they in fact live the truth which sets us free. Many of
them, however, cannot 'objectify' it, either for themselves or for
others: when they begin to reflect on what they are living discreetly and unobtrusively in the responsibility, love and loyalty of
the everyday, they find they cannot articulate it in a formal
expression of their beliefs. They become confused and begin to
doubt whether so lofty and sublime a thing as that expressed in
religious and perhaps even metaphysical statements about the
ultimate meaning of human life could exist in their lives. Perhaps
many are given only in the obscure ground of their existence what
others—religions and other interpreters of man—also dare to say
expressly. That is in principle perfectly justified, because where it
is successful it can purify and clarify the (so far unspoken) realiz-

ation of life and give courage. If this silent ground of life and its free, responsible realization is successfully interpreted in a Christian way in my present reflexions, then my subject matter concerns something that the Christian can (and even must) grant as an unreflected event even in one who in his own reflexions does not acknowledge such speech as an accurate statement of what he himself lives, or at any rate doubts the appropriateness of such discourse.

There are plenty of anguished atheists and people who doubt the eternal worth of a responsible life. Their systems, however, do not enable them to explain adequately whence such radical grief can enter the desert of existence, and their grief proclaims the opposite of what they understand in the dimension of their reflective interpretation of life. On these premises, I venture to add that where a person lives his or her life in unconditional, selfless love, in an ultimate loyalty that goes unrewarded, in responsible acceptance of the dictates of autarchic conscience—solitary and unsung as it is—he (or she) is living out a hoping belief in his permanent definitiveness, whether he reflects about it, manages to objectify this conviction verbally, or not.

Whoever stands before the graves of Auschwitz or Bangla Desh or other monuments to the absurdity of human life and manages neither to run away (because he cannot tolerate this absurdity) nor to fall into cynical doubt, believes in what we Christians call eternal life, even though his mind does not grasp it, and whether he can tolerate this statement of radical courage or not. One can live radical love, loyalty and responsibility which can never in the long run 'pay' *and* 'think' that all human life ends in the empty meaningless void, but in the very act of such a life the thought is belied, and it is contradicted by one's deeds.

Basic acts of life like these place their hope in definitiveness, in the ultimate salvation of life; they affirm the first and final condition of such hope, which we call God. Only such belief enables us to be responsible for human life, if life is otherwise doomed to perish, and prevents it from becoming no more than the fertilizer of a future which itself is destined to drop into the void. The person who says that this definitiveness is already present in life, since we become certain of God's love and faithfulness *here and now*, cannot, if he is logical, then commit such certainty to destruction. The person who experiences eternity in time must, precisely because he does so, not let destructive time carry the day over his experience of love for God and his neighbour.

We need not 'visualize' or 'picture' this definitiveness—given in radical hope—of our history and person. We know of it nothing but what is given in the unconditioned hope. We are not, of course, permitted to think of it as an extension of our time into which new things are introduced at pleasure. It is the definitiveness of our history in the presence of God, the definitiveness of a life which took place here in time, and even though in a hidden manner contained enough of what is worth existing definitively, 'for ever'. This hope applies concretely to the whole man, and consequently is already a hope for what Christians call the 'resurrection of the body'. A Platonic western tradition has been accustomed, it is true, to call the inner ground of man's permanence 'soul' and the ground of his spatio-temporality 'body', and to imagine the content of man's ultimate hope as the immortality of a *part* of man, namely his soul, and then to relegate man's 'resurrection' (of the 'flesh' which man is and not only has) as expressed in Christian hope to the end of collective history as a supervening event of consequence only to the 'body'. Today we should not criticize these Platonizing conceptual schemes too disdainfully, partly because they have constantly been used in the doctrines of the Christian Church to clarify the content of Christian teaching.

We may, however, also say that the (joint) Christian and human *hope* concerns the salvation of the entire person and therefore is a hope which cannot first of all exclude the 'body' and then learn something about *its* destiny only from a special, separate doctrine. This may be said even though we do not need to deny that the one definitiveness of man must be thought of as taking effect variously, depending on the several aspects it contains, without our being able to picture this difference perhaps of 'glorification' of 'body' and 'soul' more precisely. Ultimately, therefore, it is not a question of faith whether what we call the resurrection of the body in the narrower sense takes place at the end of collective history or is thought of as a simultaneously occurring moment of the one process by which a man achieves his definitiveness at the time of (his own) death. As early as the middle ages, theology could conceive of a 'resurrection' of man independently of the question of what happened to the corpse left behind in death. Man is one, he has a hope for himself, this hope is radically posited in the act of responsible assumption of his existence and enters the reflecting consciousness in what we call the 'resurrection of the flesh' (and also embraces the 'soul' in the latter's redeemed, beatific immortality).

It is only in such hope that we can treat of the question of Jesus' resurrection. Such hope is the locus of this latter belief. The hope at the heart of existence (it is indifferent here whether it is made one's own in freedom or rejected in despair, which is a real possibility even though it mean's man's perdition) scans history for its tangible pledge; for the event in which it can dare to say: something happened there which I hope also happens to me; for the event in which it is offered its own self-objectification and from which it draws the courage to confess itself. Christian faith finds this event in Jesus. Hope for us is a hope which, in denying Jesus, would disown itself.

This is not the place to set out everything the Christian faith professes about Jesus. We can only say briefly that faith presents this Jesus, his life, his work, his claim on us, and affirms: he lives. His cause did not perish, was not invalidated by his death. If he himself had perished, if he were not alive now, his cause would be not he himself but a mere ideology which we could have even without him. We could not call this event, of which our hope is in constant quest, Jesus, unless reports had come down to us through the apostolic witness to him, his work, his life and death and his definitive permanence in life (called resurrection). Even given all this, we can experience for ourselves in our encounter with him that he lives: in the liberating power of his life and death which took place in God, and in the testimony of his Spirit, without which we could not believe, even in his resurrection. We are not (and could not be) as dependent on the 'eyewitness' of the first disciples as those people who learn only by report of an event which occurred quite outside the circle of their own experience. The evidence of the disciples *and* our own inner evidence of the experience of the living power of Jesus (of Jesus, not of an ideology associated arbitrarily with his name in the final analysis) together form one testimony: he lives. Some people say with a shrug of the shoulders that they experience in themselves nothing of this witness of Jesus' 'Spirit' who witnesses to him as living. Those people are to be asked whether they have ever willingly exposed themselves to Jesus' challenging call which concerns life and death (that is, love for God and man in one) and then is experienced as inseparable from his person.

With regard to what is usually meant by Jesus' resurrection, we know no more that what we hope for ourselves: the permanent, effective saving of his life through God. We do not need to visualize to ourselves the peculiar nature of his physical risen existence, because we cannot. Nor do we need to see in the 'empty tomb', which could not on its own guarantee any resurrection, the proper reason for belief in his resurrection. We could, if we were so inclined, read the reports of the risen Christ's appearances in Scripture as secondary clarifications of an appearance of the risen Jesus

which properly lies *behind* these visions, because we do not have
to put these visions on a par with the kind of visions familiar to us
from the history of mysticism.

We do not regard the resurrection as an event that takes place
only in our faith; but we do say that it belongs to the permanent
victory of Jesus and his cause that it must be perpetuated in our
faith. If his resurrection was nowhere going to find faith, it would
never have happened, because it was to be God's victorious self-
promise to the world. In any case, Jesus' resurrection is not the
return of a deceased man to our space and time with all its limitations, it is something quite different of its very essence from the
raisings of dead people to life recorded in both Old and New
Testaments.

The risen Jesus announces the fact that he has been saved for
ever and his life accepted by God, but he does not return to the
world which stands under the law of fruitlessness and death and
must be conquered with our hope. We simply look on this living
and dying of Jesus's, as the first disciples did, experience his liberating power in us and then say: we should be denying our own hope
of resurrection if we did not affirm of *this* Jesus that he lives, that
he is therefore risen, if therefore our own hope did not know that
it was empowered and liberated in him for that act in which man
also accepts his ineradicable hope in freedom and lets it enter his
consciousness. As far as other people are concerned, if we take the
guilt in man's life as seriously as the hope, we should not perhaps
dare to believe in a beatific redemption of life, even though we,
the guilty, must fear more for *ourselves* than for others, whose
guilt we can never know so well as our own. If, however, there has
ever lived a person whose courage confutes the sceptical opinion
that man, so questionable and evil, should be wiped off the face
of the earth as soon as possible as a failed experiment, that person
is, according to the evidence of Christianity and way beyond the
frontiers of ecclesial Christendom, Jesus. One may even say, if
one so wishes: He must be God for the life of this Jesus not to
have foundered. Why should this life not give as good a 'proof of
God's existence' as the world, in which atoms conduct their
ghostly dance by 'chance and necessity' and man lives as a frightful question?

It can, of course, be asked what sort of situation man is in if
ultimately everything is based 'merely' on hope, and even Jesus's
resurrection is based in the final analysis 'only' on the hope in
which we also hope for everything for ourselves. To this we may
reply with unimpeachable logic that the ultimate in man as a
complete person (unlike the functional satisfaction of particular

needs in life) consists in the movement which we call hope. Hope sustains, gives reality, *when* and as it happens. And outside itself it needs no justification. Apart from hope there is only despair. We can certainly try to dismiss despair and suppress it, but without hope it is sure to return, and without freely accepted hope it does return. And despair has no justification in itself, even though it might often seem easier to man than hope, because in despair man has only to let himself fall. We may ask: Where, then, does this hope in the resurrection exert its world-shaping and world-conquering power, when, despite all the Christians who pretend they hope (but then stop all too willingly at the tangible which one can possess even without hope), human history is still a hopeless mixture of stupidity, evil and death and against it we can do no more than squeeze by in the enjoyment of the higher or lower ephemeralities?

That, however, is to miss the real question of hope. The person who asks such a question wishes not to hope but to enjoy now what is hoped for. He wants an already transformed world, not to work the transformation of the world by his hope against hope (as scripture puts it). He in his turn must be asked where his alternative is (one that can serve as a life principle), and he should ask himself whether in the final analysis he does not still accept a world which seems tolerable to him because in it other people still hope, with or without their fully knowing it. The Christian may legitimately ask (as he must also ask himself) the person who says that his life consists in an incomprehensible 'nevertheless' of selfless love (for example, in firm certainty that this world would be a little more bearable with a little more freedom and justice) whether the reality of his life really corresponds to some extent to these heroic words, and especially whether he is also willing to summon up not only the courage of hope (which he has if he really loves) but also the courage to confess explicitly the hope he summons up covertly *if* he loves selflessly. If hope is not to belie its own essence, it can tolerate no definitive limits. But where it exists and sustains the whole man, takes the whole man out of himself into this mystery we call God, it can and must also believe in Jesus's resurrection: if it knows him and if it does not imagine resurrection to be something that does not in fact belong to the content of the Christian Easter faith in the resurrection.

In the liturgy of the Orthodox Church (provided that it too, like our own Church in all too many cases—through our own fault—has not degenerated into a philistine ritualism), believers embrace each other at the Easter vigil in tears and jubilation: Christ is risen, he is truly risen. That cannot be organized and catered for in liturgy: but on Easter night believers (that is, those who think and hope they believe, but do not know it with the same certainty) and 'unbelievers' (that is, those who think they do not have such Easter faith) embrace each other as those who hope together against all hope and despite everything. The unbeliever must be glad that his believing brother hopes he believes, even when he himself thinks he has to interpret that belief as the most prodigious moonshine (he does not thereby imagine, we trust, that his unbelief is utterly certain and reliable). And the believer must still have the courage to tell his unbelieving brother (all the time praying himself: I do have faith, help the little faith I have): the Lord is risen, he is really risen. And he may, indeed must, hope that this unbelieving brother of his is in fact a believer in the hope which is unconditionally accepted in freedom. The Christian believer may certainly not suppress the demand also to believe expressly, which is incumbent on all. But on Easter night he must be glad above all that Jesus rose among many who hope, without being able to say what has already been said by the resurrection: in other words, all that it implies.

9 The future

Planetary engineering and futurology have become possibilities and tasks. They are not only fashionable, however, but necessities if life on earth is to continue to some extent as most people want it. At the same time, we are increasingly aware, to our disappointment, that the future of individuals, of nations and of humanity ultimately escapes human planning.

Even if it were desirable for man to be able adequately to foresee and plan the course of natural and human history so that his plans, like those of a god, were worked out in real history without addition or alteration, it would still be true that no futurology—however sublime and whatever the conceivable possibilities it contemplates—could spare man, even in a fulfilment such as there has never been before, the fact that ultimately he is moving into an unknown future.

Whether in his pride he sees in the unforeseeable and incalculable nature of his future the necessary space for his own creative freedom, or he suffers it as the bitterness of his finite existence, the fact is that man cannot foresee his future. What he foresees is either an abstract of possibilities from which he will only later choose in (unpredictable) freedom, or the light of a proximate dawn, which, if really fore*seen*, already belongs to his present.

If by 'future' we mean not just the day about to dawn but several decades ahead, the future remains obscure despite all the ambivalent possibilities we can foresee in it. A planetary formula intended to create the world in the concrete cannot be executed by man, in this world, with the partial material of the world. The subject of freedom in choosing from the preordained possibilities cannot adequately reflect on the preordained conditions of his own freedom. Even if he were truly free; even if he were faced with several possibilities and in an obvious situation of freedom, the ultimate aims and norms of all behaviour would still apply.

The future cannot be explored ultimately. The action of finite freedom takes place as uncontrollable destiny.

What is a man to do if he can neither be innocently absorbed in his present nor believe in a future which he can foresee and mould? What is he to do if he understands that he is not ultimately in control of world order? Should he try to enjoy the present innocently? Should he await apocalyptic horrors as certain to happen, remembering that when they do, they will make his manipulation of the future superfluous? Should he act the Promethean and claim a future as unconditionally his own creation, even if it were his heroic downfall? Is there an intelligible way for man to relate to his future?

If there is none or if it is not to be just another ideology for the control of the future, what is the prospect for man as he asks about his future? He obeys the command of the present moment, because there he is always offered several possibilities which he has to consider carefully. He plans the future in so far and as well as he can. He enjoys the present and accepts care for the future in so far as it is entrusted to him. He is calm in everything. He lets the enjoyed present disappear into an unknown future. He never exaggerates his responsibility for the future.

But that calmness is not a stoical formula by which he secretly becomes the unassailable lord of his destiny. There really is a surrender embracing both action and passion which is granted to man; it is not perfected ideology. In that surrender, full of silent hope, the Christian becomes aware of what is meant by God. But he also shares with all men everything that is human: responsible action as well as the suffering of the constant lesson that the future can never be fulfilled by man alone.